THE VIKINGS

• • • ● • ● • • •

THE VIKINGS

© **Copyright 2023 - All rights reserved.**

Published 2023 by History Brought Alive

The content contained within this book may not be reproduced, duplicated, or transmitted without direct written permission from the author or the publisher.

Under no circumstances will any blame or legal responsibility be held against the publisher, or author, for any damages, reparation, or monetary loss due to the information contained within this book, either directly or indirectly.

LEGAL NOTICE:

This book is copyright protected. It is only for personal use. You cannot amend, distribute, sell, use, quote, or paraphrase any part, or the content within this book, without the consent of the author or publisher.

DISCLAIMER NOTICE:

Please note the information contained within this document is for educational and entertainment purposes only. All effort has been executed to present accurate, up-to-date, reliable, complete information. No warranties of any kind are declared or implied. Readers acknowledge that the author is not engaged in the rendering of legal, financial, medical, or professional advice. The content within this book has been derived from various sources. Please consult a licensed professional before attempting any techniques outlined in this book.

By reading this document, the reader agrees that under no circumstances is the author responsible for any losses, direct or indirect, that are incurred as a result of the use of the information contained within this document, including, but not limited to, errors, omissions, or inaccuracies.

FREE BONUS FROM HBA: EBOOK BUNDLE

Greetings!

First of all, thank you for reading our books. As fellow passionate readers of History and Mythology, we aim to create the very best books for our readers.

Now, we invite you to join our VIP list. As a welcome gift, we offer the History & Mythology Ebook Bundle below for free. Plus you can be the first to receive new books and exclusives! Remember it's 100% free to join.

Simply scan the QR code down below to join.

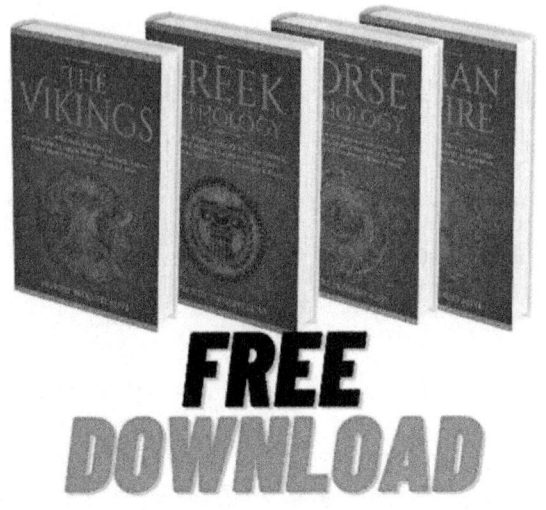

https://www.subscribepage.com/hba

Keep up to date with us on:
YouTube: History Brought Alive
Facebook: History Brought Alive
WWW.HISTORYBROUGHTALIVE.COM

CONTENTS

INTRODUCTION 1

AUTHOR BIO 6

CHAPTER 1: THE AGE OF THE VIKINGS – A TIMELINE... 10

THE BEGINNING OF THE RAIDS 11

CHAPTER 2: CULTURE AND CUSTOMS.......... 24

COMMON MISUNDERSTANDINGS ABOUT THE VIKINGS ..25
CUSTOMS IN VIKING CULTURE 29
VIKING CLOTHING 41
VIKING ARCHITECTURE 48
VIKING ART...53
DAILY VIKING LIFE... 61

CHAPTER 3: GEOGRAPHY AND REGIONAL CUISINE... 70

VIKING FOODS IN DIFFERENT REGIONS 76

CHAPTER 4: BELIEFS, MYTHS AND MYTHOLOGY.. 86

THE BEGINNING OF THE UNIVERSE............................... 88
VIKING GODS AND GODDESSES 89
PAGANISM IN VIKING CULTURE 94
CHRISTIAN BELIEFS IN VIKING CULTURE 97
THE SAGAS AND WHAT THEY TELL US 98
VIKING MYTHOLOGY AND FOLKLORE 102

CHAPTER 5: THE VIKING ARMY AND FAMOUS BATTLES...116

FAMOUS VIKING WARRIORS 128
FAMOUS VIKING BATTLES.. 133

CHAPTER 6: VIKING LANGUAGE **140**

CHAPTER 7: WHAT HAPPENED TO THE VIKINGS? **154**

    FACTORS LEADING TO VIKING DECLINE 155
    THE FINAL YEARS OF VIKING DOMINANCE 160
    THE AFTERMATH OF VIKING EXPANSION 161
    WHERE ARE THE VIKINGS TODAY? 162

CONCLUSION **165**

REFERENCES **171**

INTRODUCTION

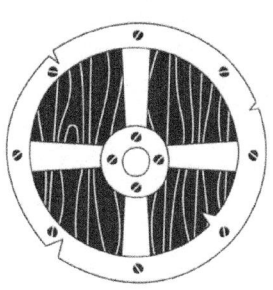

In the centuries following the fall of the Roman Empire, many civilizations, nations, and kingdoms came and went. But in 700 AD, a tribe of warriors left their homeland and struck out for glory and for conquest. They came to take no prisoners. Their eerie horns made a distinctive sound, and their fearsome longboats struck from out of nowhere; out of the fog and the gloom from the North leaving devastation in their wake. They were the Norsemen, more commonly known as Vikings, a group of men dedicated to expansion and conquest. However, the Vikings were not all about raping and pillaging. Their impact and legacy can be seen in every facet of the cultures they encountered. Many people misunderstand their cultural and historical significance in light of modern society. There is a tendency to view them as backward, unsophisticated, or mindless killers. Nothing could be further from the truth. This historical guide to the Vikings will examine what they contributed to the cultures they came into contact with, and the biggest impact that they had on European medieval society and beyond.

The name Viking comes from the Old Norse for "pirate raid." Although many did indeed raid the coastlines of European countries, they did not all have the same purpose. Some simply wanted to trade and settle in these more southern regions. Many settled in the European countries that they landed in and became citizens of those countries. They both took on the cultures of those countries and imparted their own ways and mannerisms onto these cultures. This book aims to focus on who these men and women were, and what their lives were like.

What did Vikings eat, and what did they think about the world they lived in? Food was central to the Viking culture. It formed the basis for their celebrations, rituals, and their daily lives. One could never say that they were ever timid around their food. They needed all the energy they could get in order to keep up with their daily activities, which included travelling, farming, working on the land harvesting crops, hunting, fighting, and many other activities. The Vikings, as is well-known, were seafaring people. It is important to know how their diet was impacted by their trade, industry, and expansion into other parts of the world. Vikings saw the world through the perspective of their current needs and desires. They were focused on subsistence and expansion.

What did they believe? The Vikings had their own set of beliefs and different deities that they worshipped. The worship of these gods and goddesses formed the basis of their activities as a society. Their beliefs affected their perspective of birth, death, and the afterlife. It is interesting to see what the Vikings believed about the world because it shows how their beliefs impacted the collective consciousness of Europe at the time. Traces of their systems of living and seeing the world still persist, even to this day. Much like the Vikings themselves, their legacy was built to endure throughout generations.

What was their culture like? Viking culture was intertwined with their belief systems. How they chose to live their lives was determined, to a large extent, by how they saw the world. Different times of the year were dedicated to different feast days. In battle, their warrior spirit shone through because of their emphasis on a proud and fierce patriotic sense of camaraderie. Different seasons were seen as either bountiful or cursed by the gods in times of plenty or in times of scarcity. The Vikings viewed the world in an almost mystical sense and were always on the lookout for omens and signs. This guide will dive into the vast and complicated network of their mythologies, beliefs, and ideas about the natural and spiritual world.

Most importantly this book looks to answer the question: What happened to the Vikings, and where did they go? If you go to Scandinavia today, you might find traces of the old Viking culture still there if you look hard enough! There are ancient ruins, buildings, books, and literature that testify to the great and glorious past of the Viking people. In fact, the people are the most interesting products of this era. You can learn a lot by talking to passionate Scandinavian historians themselves. But by and large, society has moved on from the age of the Vikings. Or have they? This book illustrates the ultimate fate of this richly nuanced—and often misunderstood—society.

If you want to find out more about the Vikings, this book is the definitive guide for you. It will look at the culture, life, and practices of the Vikings in a new and refreshing light. It will challenge you to see things from their perspectives. Moreover, it looks at their legacy and what we can learn from their lives.

Author Bio

History Brought Alive reveals new insights into this fascinating culture. If you want to discover more about this interesting civilization, look no further. This is the definitive guide for you. This is a reference you will want \to use over and over again. You will be amazed at the depth of knowledge present in these pages. It is a well-researched and thoroughly documented guide to the life and times of the Vikings, and puts forward the facts in a way that forces the reader to think differently about what is commonly known by Viking and Norse culture. Be prepared to tackle the subject of the Vikings with an open mind, and you'll be

surprised at how much you can learn. Much like the Vikings themselves, the reader has to be prepared to expand their way of thinking in order to appreciate the intricacies of ancient and complex cultures.

CHAPTER 1
THE AGE OF THE VIKINGS – A TIMELINE

• • • • ● • ● • • •

The Beginning of the Raids

The period of the Vikings is thought to have begun after the reign of Germanic warlords and barbarians in Europe, and about 200 to 300 years after the fall of the Roman Empire. The world had vastly changed at this point, after thousands of years of Roman rule. From around the year 793, bands of warriors began to make their way south, striking out from their native lands of what is today known as Norway, Sweden, Denmark, and the surrounding territories. Following the period commonly referred to today as the "Germanic Iron Age", people from the Nordic countries (known as Norsemen) made use of rivers around Europe to facilitate trade, travel, raids, and conquest. It was the latter of these activities that they would become most noted for.

Much of what is known about the Viking Age is based on what was written down during this period, and long after it as well, by ancient historians and experts on ancient cultures. What we learn from these records depends on who wrote down the tales of these people. If you only read the Viking records they wrote themselves, you'll get a one- sided view, as is the case if you consult the records of the people they attacked and raided. Everyone has a different view of events. It is only through a holistic view of events that the truth about this age can be properly realized.

The Vikings were not one unified group of people, although the all-inclusive term "Vikings magnat" seems to categorize them all into a single ethical or racial group. The truth is that they were a group made up of a myriad of smaller ethic groups from various Scandinavian countries such as Norway, Denmark, Sweden, and other surrounding regions. Vikings did not only come from Scandinavia, however. There are historical records of many other kinds of Vikings, such as people from Finland, Estonia, and Lapland, along with the Kola peninsula of Russia.

Let's look at where these various groups went when they left their homeland in these territories. Bear in mind that these regions were not called by their modern names until very much later on. The Danes struck out from Denmark and immediately travelled west along the North Sea to the coast of France. They landed in Spain and made sorties into the Mediterranean, and even raided a small territory in Italy called Luna, thinking that this was the seat of the Roman Empire. The Swedes sailed up towards the Baltic sea and established the Kievan Russian state, and also to the territory of the Byzantine empire and beyond, in the Orient itself. The Norwegians sailed west towards British territory, the Scottish regions, and Ireland. Dublin itself was set up as a base for slave trading in 841. Overall, these men and women spread across much of the known world, taking whatever they wished, whenever they needed it.

Apart from trade, these groups of people had little to do with each other and certainly did not present a united front. In fact, they often fought each other over scarce land, spoils, and resources. However, the Vikings were united in the eyes of the people they attacked and conquered. They were a universally feared group. They had learned the art of shipbuilding and sail-making by observing what the Romans did during the time of their empire many years before. Celtic and Germanic merchants interacted with the Romans in around 300 to 400 AD and studied their technology (Mark, 2018). It was this influence of the Romans which led the Vikings to try and grow their own navy many years later. From modern-day excavations, it is clear that the Vikings and their ancestors had held an interest in sea-related technology for a very long time. Their ancestral activities can be traced back many thousands of years before the Vikings even came to be, and this can be proven by examining the evidence of rock carvings from about 4000-2000 BC.

It is worth noting that trade between the European mainland and Germanic or barbarian traders had been taking place since Roman times. Viking furs, whetstones, and other resources had always been passing between the two groups. This, of course, led the would-be raiders to the European shores and the promise of new and fertile land for them. They saw the land they came into contact with as being ripe with opportunity for the establishment of a new civilization.

Further Expansion

In 791 AD, small raids on British monasteries began because these were often solitary and unprotected. In addition to this, these monasteries often contained a large amount of money or gold. One of the most significant of these raids was in 793 in a place called Lindisfarne.  The monastery at Lindisfarne was considered to be the center of Christianity in the region of Northumbria. It was not, however, the first raid on British territories in the British Isles. In 787, three Viking warships appeared off the coast of Wessex travelling down from a place called 'Hørthaland', in what is known as modern-day Norway today. The men on the coast of Wessex who were there at the time had expected that these ships would be willing to engage in friendly trade, but they were sorely mistaken. Further attacks occurred at the monastery of Iona in Scotland, Jarrow in Northumbria, and at various locations off the coast of Ireland in the

790s.

The Vikings left no one that they encountered alive. Their objective was to gain as much loot as they could and get back to their ships. They often burned the buildings they encountered, which included the churches they came into contact with. This is documented in the account of the raid at Lindisfarne. Many other churches along the British coastline suffered the same fate. Such was the pattern of the Viking attacks during the early years of their reign of terror.

Europe Resists

The attacks didn't stop in the 9th century. In 840, the Vikings raided territories in Ireland and established the slave colony of Dublin. During this time, they set up camps in this region and began to establish a presence in the area. Paris, in France, was attacked by the Danes in 845 and sacked. It was attacked by them again in 860. In 844, the Vikings had relocated as far south as the Spanish coastline, where they came into contact with Muslims currently living there. Sailing up the river Guadalquivir towards Seville, they were attacked by Islamic troops there and forced backwards. After this reverse, Viking raids on the Spanish territories were few and far between.

In 866, Vikings raided the north of England and established the Kingdom of York. Unusually, though, the two kings of that region—Aelle and Osbert—were not harmed or captured.

In 872, Harald Hårfagre became the first king of Norway according to Viking literature. He would rule until around 930 and is considered to be the king responsible for the unification of Norweigan tribes after the great battle of Hafrsfjord.

Following the traumatic earlier raids on their country and the overwhelming numbers of invaders running riot across their land, the English forces attempted to fight back at the battle of Edington in 878, and formulated what was known as the Danelaw in Northern England. This was an agreement allowing the Vikings to settle on various parts of English soil, where their customs took precedence over English statutes in those regions. Even in spite of their limited successes, the British Isles experienced tremendous hardship at the hands of the Vikings, and never gained true authority during these times. The Vikings eventually settled on foreign soil and established themselves there. However, more attacks from the invaders were still forthcoming.

In the year 900, the Vikings had moved as far east as they would eventually reach. On the way, they began to raid Mediterranean territories and came into conflict with the Byzantine army and navy. Under the leadership of Olef the Wise, they reached as far as Istanbul whereafter, having been paid a substantial sum of money, they decided to turn around and leave again.

Paris had been besieged in the 9th century, and it was attacked again in 911. Under the leadership of Viking Chief Rollo, they managed to forcibly gain territory in France. The descendants of Chief Rollo became the formidable force later known as the Normans. These warriors would play a huge role in shaping the outcome of English and British culture for centuries to come, although they didn't know it yet.

In 910, the Vikings were defeated at the battle of Tettenhall and Wedfield by the forces of Mercia and Wessex. In 915 and 918, the Viking King Rægnald defeated the Scots on the river Tyne. It was during these years that the Vikings began to move away from an expansionist mindset, and more towards a way of life that favored establishment of a culture and civilized life.

In the 11th century (around the year 1000), the Vikings strengthened their grip on mainland Europe, the British Isles, and made inroads into the Americas and the New World for the first time. At this time, the British tried to sue for peace with their oppressors, but they only ended up making a bad situation worse. This led to the massacre of many innocent people when they engaged in ethnic cleansing against the local population, who had settled on the coast after the arrival of the Vikings.

In 981, Erik the Red had discovered the New World after being expelled from Norway and settling in Greenland for a number of years. Within about 20 years of his landing there, about 3000 people of Norse descent now lived in this New World. They were mainly peaceful farmers and shepherds.

The Influence of Christianity

It was about the time of the turn of the millennium when the first seeds of Christianity began to be sown into the Viking culture. In 995, King Olav Tryggvasson constructed the first church on Norweigan soil. He survived being gravely injured in battle, and then returned to Norway where he attempted to introduce Christianity to the region. He might have been amongst the first Viking converts to the religion. In the year 1000, Christianity officially arrived in Iceland and Greenland when a chieftain known as King Olav took it upon himself to try and proselytize and convert fellow chieftains. He imposed trade embargoes upon those who refused to convert.

Christianity was one of the major issues that affected the development of the Viking way of life and way of thinking. A king named Haakon the Good attempted to spread Christianity to the mainland Viking community after his experiences in England, but he was unable to make much headway. King Harald Greycloak attempted to force the Vikings to acknowledge the Christian God by destroying all Viking pagan temples, but he encountered strong resistance from the people and communities that he tried to convert.

The Last Years

The age of the Vikings began to wane after the turn of the millennium due to their dispersal throughout the world and a change in their expansionist mindset. The settlement in the New World, now called 'Vinland', was abandoned due to the difficulty of receiving supplies from Europe, and the dangers of transporting goods while crossing the ocean from Scandinavia.

In 1066, the King of England at the time, Harold Godwinson, defeated the Norweigan ruler Harald Hardråda at the battle of Stamford Bridge while William, the Duke of Normandy, defeated King Harold at the Battle of Hastings. Such battles were indicative of the fact that the Viking order was drawing to a close, or at least changing in a significant way. Gone were the days where the sight of their ships would cause chaos. At this time, other, more significant threats to Europe were becoming paramount. It is clear, however, that at this time, Vikings were becoming more and more integrated into European life as a whole. However, their practices and ways of living were still seen as crude and dirty by the people they came into contact with.

CHAPTER 2
CULTURE AND CUSTOMS

• • • • • • • • •

Common Misunderstandings About the Vikings

Horned Helmets

The Vikings did not often make use of horned helmets, as is commonly depicted in many forms of media. In fact, evidence of these horns has never been discovered, and Viking literature and the sagas make no mention of them at all. It is commonly believed that the idea behind horned helmets like this originated with an operatic work by Wagner in 1876 called *Der Ring des Nibelungen*. In real life, horned helmets would have made little sense in close combat. They could easily be removed and could be a danger to the wearer. In addition, they were unwieldy and likely to fall off during a fight. They would never have been used and were never used in any form of combat that the Vikings took part in.

Unified Viking State

There is the common misconception that the Vikings were part of one, large, unified state and that they all had a common goal. The reality of the situation was vastly different. There was no Viking Empire as there was with, say for example, the Romans. The Vikings were a group of people with similar interests from all over Scandinavia, who shared common customs and ways of thinking and living. There was unity of sorts when they formed the Great Heathen Army, but it seems as if such unity amongst various tribal groups was the exception rather than the norm. Their governments or leadership tended to operate on a more local level.

Being a Viking Was a Career

Many people misunderstand the nature of the Viking life. People were not born Vikings. They took this culture and way of life upon themselves when they decided to embark on a lifestyle of raiding and pillaging. They were Norse people, but Viking in occupation. Vikings themselves had their own specific cultural practices which weren't found in Norse culture, but on the whole, being a Viking was a way of life.

The Vikings Were Barbarians

A common misconception about Vikings is that they were uneducated, savage, or barbarian in nature. This is due to the fact that they (correctly) raided and pillaged, but this is not the only thing they did. Many were interested simply in finding places to live and to settle. They wanted to raise a family and survive as much of the rest of Europe was doing at that time. The reason they raided and killed was because of a constant desire for conquest and expansion, so that they could form their own settlements in the places they conquered. The Vikings were practical people. They attacked the least defended places they could find, which included lightly-guarded settlements, small towns, monasteries, and other similar buildings. Monasteries were popular because they were filled with gold and other valuable materials. Many of the people who worked at these monasteries were some of the few people who were literate at that time. Therefore, the written records of Viking activity were generally of these raids and events. These records have contributed towards the overall image of Vikings as being fierce and doing nothing but raiding. Much less is said about their more peaceful activities.

Truth Is Stranger Than Fiction

Much of what is portrayed about the Vikings in TV and media is peculiar, and the reality is that their sagas portray a mythology that is much stranger than anything that could be shown on screen. For example, Loki is currently a popular character due to various movies and TV shows that have featured him. But his history and backstory is quite outlandish. He has been known to have given birth to an eight-legged horse, for example. He is also the father of a massive serpent and a giant wolf. None of this makes a great deal of sense to the uninitiated, but this is the strangeness, and the appeal, of Viking mythology in a nutshell. It is not to be understood, but experienced.

Viking Funerals

There is a common misconception that Vikings were always given the traditional Viking funeral, which involved placing the remains of the body in a boat and sending them off on the sea. This, however, did not take place that often. Viking ships were expensive and time-consuming to build, and they did not want to be breaking or destroying anything without good reason. It seems that Viking boat burials were instead reserved for the most important members of their societies. The Vikings had a variety of other funeral practices for others, which depended on their gender, social status, and military status.

The Vikings Were Only In Scandinavia

The Vikings travelled all over the world. They went to Canada, the United Kingdom, the British Isles, and all over Europe. There is no account that states that they were exclusively from Scandinavia, although this was where many Viking groups were active. Their presence in Europe was widespread.

Customs in Viking Culture

Social Structure

Viking society, depending on the region, was organized under more or less a strict social and patriarchal structure. There were three main classes in Viking society: Earls (*jarlar* in Old Norse), free men, and slaves. Earls were the upper class in society and received the greatest benefits. Many of these men were warlords and warriors who had obtained their success through being victorious in battle. When Viking territories became kingdoms, these earls became second only to the kings in these regions.

The majority of people fell into the second class, the free men (*karlar* in Old Norse). Most of these men and women were farmers and worked on the land. Others were content to labor for farmers within a kind of feudal system. Some worked at creating weapons, crafts, and other items. Free men on the land enjoyed the protection of legal systems, unlike those who were slaves.

Viking warriors often belonged to the free men. They were warriors who, although not at the very top of the social hierarchy in Viking society, enjoyed reasonable standing within the community. They had little wealth but were sometimes alloted portions of land that they could use to feed themselves and their families. Many, however, were unmarried. Due to their single status, they were able to act in whatever way they pleased without fear of social ostracization.

The final group were the slaves or the poorest class (*þrælar* in Old Norse). These men usually carried out the most menial of tasks and could be bought or sold. Female slaves were cooks, concubines and domestic workers. They lived in the houses of more wealthy people. Slaves were often born into their status and remained there their entire lives. When a wealthier master died, their slaves were often sacrificed and then buried with them. Slaves were also made up of those who were captured during Viking raids. Because these men were not killed and were instead spared, they often had to pay back their captors by serving them their entire lives. Men could also become slaves through declaring bankruptcy as it was the only way they could survive and have somewhere to live.

Birth

The birth of any child within Viking society was a celebrated event, and was seen as a positive sign. The birth of sons was particularly auspicious. Before a child was born, songs were sung about the birth as a way of ensuring that the mother and child would remain safe and secure during the birthing process. Nine days after delivery, the father of the child would take the infant and place them on his knees, where water was sprinkled on the child's head. Guests were invited to the ceremony, and gifts were exchanged amongst the participants.

Marriage

Marriage was another celebrated event within Viking societies. A marriage could only take place if both the families of the bride and groom agreed on specific terms, such as property rights and a dowry for the bride. Viking weddings were meticulously planned events. A father would take his daughter around town so that she could be seen by other people and men in the town. Once they had gained the attention of a man, he would have to approach her family, and the two families would have to agree terms. Certain issues had to be worked out, such as the *mundr* (bride price), *heiman flygia* (dowry), and *morgedn-gifu*, which were morning gifts that were bestowed to the bride by the groom on the morning of the wedding itself. Once this contract was finalized, the marriage could proceed. A groom could be married to a bride after he proposed to her, accompanied by his family. When the proposal was accepted by the bride and ratified by the family, preparations for the event could start to take place. The day itself was accompanied by massive feasts and festivals that could last for days. Once vows were exchanged, it was considered customary for witnesses to accompany the newly-wedded couple to their bed on the wedding night.

Frigga was the Viking goddess of marriage, and it was considered to be lucky to hold the wedding ceremony on her holy day, known as "Frigga's Day" or Friday. Preparations for the wedding included gathering and preparing enough food and large supplies of alcohol for the celebration. A massive quantity of honey mead was consumed during the celebration along with the food. It was considered compulsory for the bride and groom to partake in the honey mead or ale at the wedding ceremony, and also during the month that followed the wedding. Weddings were also traditionally held after the harvest and before the long, cruel, and dark winter months where it would be considered to be difficult to be outside in any capacity. Guests would also not be able to travel during this period, so it was essential that wedding ceremonies be held when the weather was fine.

The bride would be prepared by her friends, bridesmaids, mother, and other married women. She would remove the *kransen,* or golden circlet, that she carried in her hair as a sign that she was ready to be married. This golden circlet would be worn her entire life and passed on to her daughter, if she had one, in order to maintain the family line. In such a way, this Viking tradition was maintained throughout the centuries. Following the ceremony, the golden circlet would be replaced with one made of silver or woven wheat or straw. The bride would bathe and be instructed in her new duties by her maids, servants or attendants.

As far as the groom was concerned, there were also ceremonies that needed to be carried out. One of the most interesting of these was that of breaking and entering the grave of an ancestor in order to retrieve a sword that belonged to a long dead relative. This symbolized his entering into the realms of death and emerging as a man, his boyhood left behind. He would then get dressed and be instructed by wiser and older men in his duties as a husband (Bartley, 2018).

The ceremony itself was simple. The groom would present his bride with the ancestral sword he had retrieved, which she kept to pass along to her son in later years. She would present him with the sword of her own ancestors. Rings attached to the hilts of their swords were then exchanged between the couple.

After this, the groom would walk or ride to the feast venue and stand in the doorway with his sword across it, blocking the bride from entering. He would then carry her across the threshold himself. What followed were several days of feasting, jokes, laughter, drinking, and merriment. Wrestling contests also took place at the feast, and everyone had a good time.

The final part of the ceremony involved being parted for a short time on the morning after the wedding night. The bride was prepared and her hair was styled in a specific fashion by her attendants. She wore a linen head covering as a symbol of her new status in marriage. She was then escorted into a hall where a number of onlookers were waiting along with the groom. There, she would be presented with the morning gift from the groom. Before all the witnesses, the final act for the contract of marriage to be complete was performed. The husband then took the keys to his residence and gave them to her as a way of showing her authority over all things related to the home.

Death

Unravelling the way the Viking's responded to death in their culture is a complex matter. Inconsistency is abundant within their sagas and Viking literature of the time. Because written accounts span several centuries, opinions on this issue, the ultimate end of human life, tend to vary considerably. However, there are certain patterns that we as amateur historians can use to draw certain conclusions. One thing is for certain, the Vikings did indeed believe in the existence of an afterlife, and this is evident throughout their literature. As for the beliefs of pagan Viking religion, they are difficult to decode, as little is written about them in Viking literature itself. It is therefore incumbent upon historians to try and piece together fragments of what we know about Viking life and their ways of thinking. How did they approach the issue of dying? What were their funerals like? What were their attitudes towards death?

From what we know of Viking religion, it was like a personal and private belief system which amounted to small groups of people who believed similar things, and families who had shared values of how they saw the world.

Vikings believed in cremating their dead,

and this was an important process after death. When they died naturally or in battle, they were buried with the items that were most important to them while they were still alive. This included their weapons and jewelry. It was thought that they would need specific items when they went into the afterlife. Oftentimes, a Viking would be buried with the items that most represented who they were in life, for example weapons for warriors and clothing and other items for women. The wealthiest of Vikings might be buried in a ship that they could use in the afterlife, or the outline of a ship would be drawn on the ground and the body placed in the middle of it. Other wealthy Vikings were often buried with their slaves as these were seen as being part of the wealthy Viking's possessions. Some outsiders and observers to Viking funerals have reported on the rare occasion that young women were sacrificed at the funeral of Viking chieftains, but little is known as to whether this was customary or even an accurate representation of what took place at that time.

Many people, when they hear the words 'Viking' and 'afterlife' together, think of Valhalla, and the famous stories of Viking warriors who nobly died in battle so that they could obtain the honor of going there. However, this is only one very small part in the much larger framework of what Vikings believed about the afterlife. The reality is a lot more complicated. In ancient Nordic beliefs, it was thought that a person was composed of four different parts: *Hamr* (physical appearance), *Hugr* (personality), *Fylgja* (essence or totem), and *Hamingja* (quality or inherent success throughout one's life). When a Viking died, it was thought that their *Hamr* passed away and disappeared, while their *Hugr* passed into the afterlife. Their *Hamingja* was what remained on earth after they were gone, and this was why the Vikings put such a great deal of emphasis on the need for retaining family customs throughout the centuries.

According to Viking literature and mythology, there were several places that the *Hugr* part of the person could find themselves after they died. By far the most well-known of these places was the legendary 'Valhalla.' Valhalla was considered to be a kind of hall in the mystical land of Asgard where the great Viking god Odin lived. Odin was the king of all the Viking gods, and he was also the god of war and of wisdom. In Valhalla, there would be constant feasting, fighting, and celebration for all eternity—or until the end of the world, when the great, devastating event would take place called 'Ragnarok' (the end of all things). Only the most famous and bravest of Vikings could end up in Valhalla, and one would have to perform certain feats of extreme valor during one's life in order to be allowed to enter.

The next realm was called 'Folkvangr', or the realm of the goddess Freya. She was the goddess of fertility and magic. It was her job to gather all the dead heroes from the battlefield and bring them to her realm. Although it is less well-known than Valhalla, Folkvangr seems to hold a higher prestige in Viking literature than Valhalla. Only the greatest of Viking heroes were allowed entrance. Like the Vikings in Valhalla, the men in this place would be allowed to take part in the final battle to end all battles at Ragnarok.

The next location is known as 'Helheim.' This was the region given to those who did not die in battle. It was located beneath the region of 'Midgard' and is also ruled over by the goddess known as 'Hel.' This realm is separated from the realm of the living by a river that cannot be crossed by those either living or dead. It is worth noting that this region was not for the souls of the wicked. That the region was known as 'Nastrond', or the realm of those who had no honor in life, and were rejected after death because of their actions.

'Ran' was the name of the next region. It was a special place in the afterlife reserved for sailors. Sailors who drowned would encounter the goddess known as Ran, after which the region is named. She kept large amounts of treasure there, and would capture the souls of dead sailors in large nets and imprison them.

The next region was known as 'Helgafjell.' This was a region located on top of a high mountain where the souls of the good sometimes ended up. Sometimes people going there would end up with their families, and it was considered to be a place of peace and serenity.

Finally, there were the traditional Christian views of Heaven (the abode of good people after they died) and Hell (the abode of the wicked). It is uncertain how much Christianity influences Viking beliefs as a whole. But one thing is for certain, Viking culture did believe in the afterlife, and as time went on, their beliefs evolved to become more like Christianity in many ways.

Ancestor Worship

The Vikings valued their ancestral ties, and their cultures revolved around the need to maintain them. It was believed that these ancestors were able to impact the lives of the living even after they themselves were dead. The family itself was a representation of all that the ancestors did in their lives in the past. It goes without saying that pagan religions within Viking culture tended to value the idea of ancestral worship more so than the Christian beliefs themselves.

Viking Clothing

Viking clothing was made for the climate in which the Vikings lived. It was designed to insulate the wearer against the harshest of climates. The warmest material that the Vikings had access to was wool. Hats were made of woolen materials or a fabric that kept heat in. Woolen socks kept cold feet warm in winter. Belts were made of leather or another strong fabric and held an outfit together. Knives and other tools could be hung on these belts for easy access when they were required. Clothing was dyed using vegetable juices and other natural substances. Colors could be mixed with each other to create different shades. Silk and other more expensive materials were rarer in Viking culture, but the wealthier chieftains and members of society could still afford them.

Men commonly wore a tunic across the front of the chest and women tended to wear more traditionally feminine outer garments or longer dresses. Men usually wore trousers, which could be either tight or loose fitting. There are few examples of Viking clothing from archaeological sources. This is because what was preserved has not survived the hundreds of years post-burial. Fabric and other materials tend to disintegrate over time. Much of what we know about Viking clothing comes from their own sagas and literature of the time.

The Vikings made use of clothing in many ways, even if it was worn out or damaged. Old clothing could be coated with pitch or tar and reused or used for other purposes. A Viking overtunic was known as a *kyrtill* and was constructed from a number of woolen fabric pieces intricately woven together. It resembled a long-sleeved shirt without buttons.

Under the tunic, Viking men often wore an undertunic or vest. This provided an added layer of protection for them in the winter months. This second layer of clothing would sit close to the skin, wick moisture away from the body, and provide warmth by not allowing air to escape.

Vikings wore cloaks in colder weather and sometimes when they went into battle. It is considered to be one of the more distinctive parts of Viking attire. When one thinks of a stereotypical Viking warrior, they are usually depicted with these cloaks around them. So, how were these cloaks constructed? They were commonly made from animal skins—sheepskins in particular—as these were some of the warmest materials available at the time.

Viking trousers (or pants) had no fly and no pockets. This meant that if the wearer wanted to relieve themselves, they would need to drop their pants first. Pockets were non-existent, which meant that everything that needed to be stored on a person had to be carried by means of a belt. This could be loosened when the wearer wanted to remove the pants. Women also carried their items in this way—by wearing a belt.

In battle, clothes tended to be a lot more robust. A thicker cloak or tunic could be used to ward off lighter projectiles in a pinch. Overall, Viking clothing was designed to be practical and effective for the environment that it found itself in. Tight-fitting clothing was avoided amongst many Vikings, and is referred to as restrictive in some of their sagas. The reason for this is because it was difficult to remove when the occasion demanded it. When Vikings moved down and settled in the very different climates of Europe, their styles of wearing clothes changed because their needs were different. The warmer climates no longer necessitated the use of heavier cloaks and thick tunics, for example.

Women's Clothing

Women's clothing was similar to men's in terms of the basic material used. Women tended to wear a dress typical for women during the medieval period, in a style that was popular amongst many cultures or civilizations in Europe and the surrounding areas at the time. They wore a mid or ankle-length dress with the neck closed by a brooch. There is also evidence that Viking women wore a kind of overdress which required no brooches to fasten in place.

Oftentimes, women would wear brooches which were capable of carrying multiple items on them that were needed for work. These items included needles, scissors, pins, and more. A woman would also carry a whetstone and a knife on her belt. Women also wore jewelry, including beads, earrings, and necklaces of various kinds. Wealthy Viking women could afford the most costly jewelry available. Sometimes, they were gifted these items by their more wealthy husbands or suitors. It was for this reason that a wealthy Viking husband was highly sought after by many women because of the benefits that this could offer them, such as security.

Head coverings were sometimes worn by

Viking women. These coverings included a knotted piece of square material. One special occasions, the headpieces might be more elaborate, such as when a woman got married. Sometimes, elaborate headdresses distinguished married women from unmarried ones.

Slave Clothing

Slave clothing was similar in terms of its constituent parts to that of wealthier Vikings but the nature of it was a lot simpler in style and fashion, and it was not as high in quality as the clothing afforded by wealthier people. The materials tended to differ as slaves could not afford the more expensive materials.

Making of Clothing

The making of clothes was a time-consuming process and had to be carried out by skilled members of the family. Depending on the materials being used, different processes had to be carried out. Clothes were made of natural fibres. These materials used for making clothes included the aforementioned sheep-skin, flax, silk, or various forms of linen. Women usually made the clothes, as Viking society dictated that this task would be entrusted to women, who were taught these skills from a young age. A well-made suit of clothes was considered to be costly and valuable. It would be carefully preserved and worn only on special occasions. Clothing could be dyed in various ways depending on what the need of the person wearing it was. It was considered fashionable to wear colorful clothing, and more expensive liquid could be used for dying clothes in certain colors. In many instances, dying clothes was an art form. Rich colors such as red, dark blue, purple, silver, gold, and even orange signified that the wearer was wealthy. If a garment was difficult to dye, it was left undyed. Patterned fabrics were popular throughout Viking culture and are mentioned in the sagas themselves, for example in the *Njáls* saga.

Furs

During the age of the Vikings, there was a roaring trade in furs. This is how they came into contact with people from Europe in the first place, amongst other reasons. These furs included mink, marten, bear, fox, bear, squirrel, and many other kinds of animals. Sable was also popular. It was seen as a symbol of power if one wore the skin of, for example, a bear, because it meant that you had killed that animal and you had power over it.

Viking Architecture

One of the lesser considered aspects of Viking culture and civilization is the way in which they created their buildings and edifices. Not much remains of Viking architecture these days, and what we know largely comes from the sagas and Viking literature. There are various buildings that the Vikings are most known for. We will examine two of these buildings, namely the Viking longhouse and the Viking stave church. Some of these iconic buildings are still standing today and can be viewed in Scandinavian countries.

Viking materials for building were primarily gathered from the forests of Scandinvian countries. Let us first look at the construction of Viking longhouses. These buildings were meant to be used by the community, and their design reflects this fact. According to Rouă (2016), Viking longhouses were made of wattle with thatched roofs with timber frames for support. These buildings were practical to design and easy to construct.

While wood was easy to come by in most Scandinavian countries, places like Greenland, Iceland, and the Faroe Islands found it harder to come by. These countries had to make use of alternative materials, such as turf, in order to construct warm, weather-proof houses. Sod, stone, and other materials were all used when wood wasn't available.

Longhouses were designed with a firepit in the middle and a hole above it so that the smoke could escape. In spite of the image of these longhouses as being dirty or crowded places, they were actually carefully constructed. Norse families lived in the central room of the longhouse where it was most snug. They cooked, slept, worked, and told stories in the warmest rooms. Viking longhouses were some of the cosiest places to be during the dark, cold winter months.

Some of these houses can still be seen standing today, while others have been reconstructed. These structures can be seen in places such as Borg in Norway, Hobro in Denmark, and Newfoundland in Canada. Some of these fascinating houses are considered to be world heritage sites by UNESCO and are considered to be culturally important areas.

Another noteworthy building in the context of Viking culture is the stave church, which of course, became more prominent with the advent of Christianity. These churches are interesting because of the unusual way in which they were constructed. There are many different kinds of stave churches, but what they all have in common are the fact that they are constructed with staves (posts) in the corners. The staves support a framework of timber beams, which in turn holds the plank walls upright. The walls are called stave walls and thus, this is how the church got its name. These buildings often feature ornate carvings of dragons and other animals which were commonly represented in Viking literature. The dragon, in particular, symbolizes the ferocity of the Viking mindset before the advent of Christianity. These churches are dotted through Norway, Sweden, and Denmark and can be visited to this day, as they are not unlike museums. These buildings give us great insight into what Viking life was like during these years.

According to what is known through archaeological evidence and Viking literature, they did have an understanding of town planning and architecture. While not on the level of some of the more advanced civilizations, they did have a solid grasp of the basics needed to construct a network of roads and towns, and these things are evident in the historical evidence that has been left behind by them. Examples of famous Viking towns included Hedeby in the German state of Schleswig-Holstein, Birka in Sweden, and Kaupang in Skiringssal in Norway. These towns give credence to the idea that the Vikings not only had advanced technologies for the time, but that they were able to function in a coherent way as a society, while other societies might not have coped with the hardships they were faced with.

There is evidence that the Vikings or Norsemen built a ring of fortifications around the perimeter of their land in Denmark and southern Sweden. These fortifications were known as *trelleborgs*. These circular structures not only served as defensive barriers, but they could have also served as a base for launching raids on England and Europe during the 9th and 10th century. These could have also been used for trading and other important administrative activities. Let us look at what these fortresses were like, in more detail.

Each of these forts contained numerous houses within them that could have been used to accommodate troops, slaves, and chieftains. In addition to houses, they could also contain all the other elements of typical fortified defenses, such as watchtowers, storage space for supplies, areas where weapons could be constructed, and many other features. Their uniqueness lies in the fact that they were circular, which was an unusual shape for a fortification during this era. Several of these constructions are still standing to this day and have been donated to UNESCO as a world-heritage site (Rouă, 2016).

In addition to the housing of warriors, slaves and other relevant parties, the *trelleborgs* also housed governmental officials and were a meeting point for royalty during Viking times. It was for this reason that they were heavily protected and were designed with this in mind. It was thought that the Vikings used these structures to launch attacks on the English coastline. For a long time, the English were unaware of their existence.

Viking Art

With all the talk of architecture, let us look at how this fits into the broader framework of Viking art. Architecture itself is considered a form of art, and it is interesting to see how the Viking view of the world was displayed in the way they expressed themselves through different mediums. It must be said the Viking art is amongst the most fascinating in the world, probably due to how little is known about it. Given the rough nature of Vikings, one would expect their art to be unsophisticated or crude, but the reality is very different.

Creation of highly developed and interesting objects was of great interest to the Vikings because of the nature of their mindset and civilization. Being as they were, an adventuring people, they were always trying new things and were always looking for new ways of accomplishing something. So, this is reflected in their art and creation of objects of rare sophistication and beauty. One must also remember that during this time, the Vikings were only a very small offshoot of a much larger Norse culture. The Vikings made extensive use of their resources to create these objects, making use of what they had available around them, and many of these objects still survive to this day.

One of the materials that they used most frequently was wood, as it was cheap and plentiful in the regions that they lived in. Unfortunately, wood has the tendency to disintegrate over time, and little remains of their work during this period.

Stone and other similar materials are quite a bit more durable, and it is these items which we have many of today. Metalwork, earthen vessels, and other items made of metal, clay, glass, and stone give us a great insight into the Viking way of viewing the world. The nature of many of the items is utilitarian in nature, displaying the Viking propensity for items that could be *used*. They tended to view the world and art not through aesthetic means, but valued an item for its practicality. The more functional an item was, the more valuable it was. This does not mean that they did not value aesthetics, but that aesthetics played a secondary role in many respects.

According to Snow (2020), Viking art was made up of a number of different motifs, all combining together to form a continuous whole. It was difficult to tell the end from the beginning. Imagery in Viking art reflected the times that they lived in, their social practices, mythological beliefs, and daily life. As Christianity began to make its way into Viking culture, evidence of this was seen in Viking art. Instead of being mainly focused on pagan images, it began to incorporate more Christian themes.

Beasts were a common theme in Viking art, both mythological and natural. The most well-known of these was, of course, the dragon. It is abundantly used as a symbol throughout Viking literature, their sagas, and their art. There were two kinds of beasts that were quite common, namely the "ribbon beast" and the "gripping beast." The Vikings referred to the first beast as the "ribbon beast" because it had an elongated head and simplified features (Snow, 2020). The other was known as the "gripping beast" because it had well-defined limbs and detailed features. These figures seemed to be most common in the most famous of Viking constructions, the longboat, carved in the prow of these legendary vessels. They not only struck fear into the enemy when they saw the ships coming, but they also marked the Vikings out as unique.

In order to understand a little more about how Viking art works, we can also examine the different styles into which their work is categorized. These styles are *Oseberg, Borre, Jellinge, Mammen, Ringerike,* and *Urnes.* Each of them is associated with a different time period starting from about 775 AD and ending in about 1125 AD (Snow, 2020).

Oseberg

This is a style associated with the early part of the Viking age. It was popular all over Scandinavia and not restricted to a particular localized area. One of the defining works of this period (775-875) is a specific longship, known simply as the *Oseberg* ship that was ornately carved featuring elements of the gripping and ribbon beasts in swirling motions. The burial mound where this ship was found has given rise to the name of the movement itself.

Borre

This is the second major style from the early Viking age period, and it overlaps with the first period. It lasted from around the year 850 to about 950. This style seems to have been focused around the British Isles and the Baltic region, as Vikings travelled in both directions. The *Borre* art period is characterized by the use of tightly-interlaced motifs that blot out the background, making it difficult to see. Animal motifs are more cartoonish, in a sense, than in other art styles, and classic ribbon shapes seem to be less conspicuous in this period. One of the most commonly known pieces from this period is that of a silver brooch from Gotland with a series of human and animal figures on it. The animals are portrayed as licking their backs with their tongues. Overall, the art during this period seems to focus on making its subjects appear with contorted bodies and triangular-shaped heads.

Jellinge

The next major art style has been placed at around 900 to 975. It combines many elements of the previous two styles and deals with a wide variety of subjects. The name of the style originated with the finding of a silver cup in a burial mound in Jelling, a region in Denmark. In this style, backgrounds are lighter in color and more detailed, while the creatures themselves seem to be simplified. The ribbon beasts make a return during this period. Solid colors are used for images and geometric shapes are used to show the joints between their legs and arms (in the case of humans). This is in sharp contrast to *Borre,* where spiral shapes were used to depict the lines between leg and arms, and the bodies of the creatures.

Mammen

Mammen is a unique style of Viking art spanning the years 960 to 1000, known for being associated with the Viking king Harald Bluetooth. It comprises elements of *Jellinge* style, foliate motifs, and notable influences from the European continent. The name of this style originated from the account of a ceremonial ax head that was discovered near a village in Denmark. Loops, waves, and tendrils seem to be distinctive of this particular style, as is seen in the image of a bird created in the late 10th century. It is noted for having beaded ornamentation and wings which reflect this flowing style.

Another discovery in the *Mammen* style is a set of runestones in the Jelling region. It features a creature called a "great beast" (Snow, 2020). It is meant to reflect the conquest of a great ruler during that time, and his victory in a specific battle. It has been interpreted as a symbol of power and dominance.

These stones are meant to reflect the power and dominance of Harald Bluetooth at this time, hence why they were set up. These stones also contain images of Christ himself, wrapped in tendrils as typical of this style. It is a convoluted and complex technique to unlock given the varying influences that it had had over the centuries.

Ringerike

Ringerike is characterized by its whimsical nature and its ingenuity. It lasted from around 990 to 1050, just when the Viking age was entering its declining years—or changes were taking place within the culture and civilization as a whole. While being influenced by aspects of other art styles, *Ringerike* also tries to develop a unique style of its own. Gone are the beaded ornamentations from previous periods. European influences were beginning to take over at this point, and this is evident in the use of vegetal themes in the works. Tendrils continue to make an appearance, and the style is very much more reminiscent of other, popular European works at the time.

Urnes

In the final stage of the Viking age, there is a

distinct move towards more elegant and classical European themes. The *Urnes* style lasted from around 1050 to around 1125, after which little is known of Viking art styles—at least that is recorded. It is commonly believed that even if the Viking age did not end at this point, something had been fundamentally altered in terms of their social and historical context. Europe was not the same place as it was 500 years earlier. With regards to the art style itself, it is known for its depiction of animals in a different manner. Animals were portrayed in regal poses, and anatomical features are more elongated. This style is associated with the Norweigan village of Urnes, where there is also a stave church located. Stave churches themselves, although around long before these techniques came to existence, seem to take on the artistic movements that were popular at the time.

Overall, Viking art styles demonstrate an unusual variety of color, variety, texture, and subject matter. From animal scenes to mythological beasts, to everyday living, Viking art seems to be noteworthy for its flexibility, creativity, and ingenuity. Looking at Viking art helps us understand that this society wasn't just about war, expansion, and conquest. They were people with keen and creative minds.

Daily Viking Life
Everyday Life in Viking Times

When Vikings weren't waging war in other countries, they were planting and harvesting their crops. They were primarily hunting, farming, and fishing people. Although they traded goods and services with Europe, most Norse people were subsistence farmers, which meant that whatever they grew, hunted, or killed, they used for themselves and their families. So given that their primary purpose was survival, for the most part, what did a typical day look like for someone living in Scandinavia during these times?

A day would typically begin early by getting up and milking the cows, feeding the sheep and goats, and getting the cattle out to pasture if they were wealthy enough to own a large amount of livestock. Men went to work in the fields or sent their servants to do this. Women would work on chores around the house, which included cleaning, washing, dusting, preparing and cooking food, and taking care of children (if they had any). In the midst of all these activities, breakfast would be eaten. This was known as *dagmal*. It could consist of a small amount of meaty stew left over from the night before, bread, fruit, porridge made of wheat, barley or other grains, buttermilk, and cheese. Eggs would also be consumed if they were available. *Dagmal* was eaten two to three hours after waking up, and after they had done all their chores. Vikings did not eat much in the middle of the day. The next meal they would eat would be in the evening, and it was called *nattmal*. It was a meal consisting of meat, fish, vegetables, bread, fruit, mead, and cheeses. In between these meals, Viking men would be working hard. There was not much time to do everything they needed to do, and so the daytime would be used for the most pressing of activities. When night fell, they could rest and socialize. During the day, however, farming activities such as ploughing and fertilizing would take place. This was backbreaking work, and everyone tried to do their best to contribute towards the labor effort so that the tasks could be done more quickly.

Tasks that were considered undesirable, such as constructing houses and buildings, flinging manure on fields, disposing of dead animal carcasses, old rotten food, waste from the house, and other negligible jobs were given to slaves to carry out. They were then afforded the generous protection of the household and allowed to live somewhere on the property and maybe partake in some of the food that was given out. Slave-holders did not pay their slaves any wages. However, if they sold some goods at market on the request of the master, they might be able to keep a little of the proceeds depending on the situation. These slaves were kept after raids or battles that were successful. They could earn their freedom if a master died or if circumstances changed. But usually, slaves were not sold once they were in the care of a master, unless he was somehow in financial trouble (in which case he would likely not have slaves—they were a sign of some kind of wealth).

The reality of everyday Viking life is that it was tedious and boring. The same kinds of activities had to be carried out every single day, and these tasks were time-consuming, arduous, and unexciting. Nonetheless, the Vikings had to do these things in order to survive, and it was a natural way of living for them. Famines, enemy raids, pestilence, disease, and many other dangers were also a part of their daily life, and they had to learn to cope with such situations as best they could when they arrived.

Famine and disease took their toll on the population, as did war. These elements of life were costly. The population had to adopt an attitude of acceptance when these things occurred because they understood that they had little power to stop them.

Viking Appearances

Vikings were Nordic people, often with characteristic blond hair and blue eyes, but this was not necessarily universal. Their skin was fair, and their hair color could vary between being blond, reddish blond, or extremely fair. Viking men had longer hair while slaves tended to keep their hair a lot shorter. The length of a Viking man's hair depended on what was practical or convenient at the time. For those in battle, it might not always be practical to have longer hair, so it was adjusted as needed. Women tended to keep their hair up when working and when it was important to do so, only letting it down when they no longer needed to keep it tied up. Married women often wore their hair in a bun to differentiate them from those who were unmarried. The different classes of Vikings were easy to spot by their appearance. Vikings who were more wealthy wore jewelry, ornate belts, and were well-groomed. Those in the middle class had similar tastes but expressed them in a less formal or ostentatious way. Slaves didn't have much of a choice about what to wear, and so were more simple in their manner of dressing and their appearance. The wealthiest Vikings would carry certain items with them with which to groom themselves, such as ornate combs and decorative items such as brooches. These would not be found on those who were less wealthy.

Sports and Recreation

Because physical fitness was important to the Vikings, they took part in many kinds of games and sports. These took place during the hours when they weren't doing work in the fields or whatever their daily occupation happened to be. Being a warrior culture, the Vikings took pride in their ability to overcome obstacles. Their sports reflected this. Games they played involved balancing, running, jumping over obstacles, swimming, rowing, and they had kinds of snow-related sports, such as ice skating and skiing. Mountain climbing was also popular as it built stamina and endurance.

During times when it was difficult to be outdoors, the Vikings loved board and dice games. Archaeological evidence supports this. The items used in these games were carved from wood, bone or tusks of animals such as walrus, and antlers from, for example, reindeer.

Vikings were rough during their games, and it was not uncommon for people to be hurt or killed during these rowdy activities. Vikings enjoyed a game played with a stick and ball. This game is known as *knattleikr*. It was a game popular across the region of Scandinavia and could be played in all kinds of weather if it was desired. It bears similarities to the modern-day game of hurling. Few written rules about the game survive but from what is known, it seems that it was a game played on two teams. It was a spectacular game, played from the morning until evening, and much like our sporting events today, it was quite the spectacle. The ball was struck with a stick or any other part of the body. There were penalty boxes and penalties were given. It seems as if the more aggressive players tended to be more successful, and there are several instances where a war of words broke out in the game and physical fights occurred. A smooth surface was required to play the game, be it sand, dirt, or ice.

The game has been revived in modern-day society and is played amongst some adherents of Viking customs.

Social Activities

Social activities often revolved around food, as this was central to the Viking of thinking. Happy times were celebrated with feasting, drinking, and dancing. Storytelling, poetry, music, and other forms of visual or auditory arts were popular at social gatherings. Music in particular was an art form for the more wealthy in society, as only highly skilled people could play instruments, such as the lyre and lute. This was because only wealthy people could afford to be trained, or had the time for such activities. Those who were poorer could not because they had neither the money nor the time.

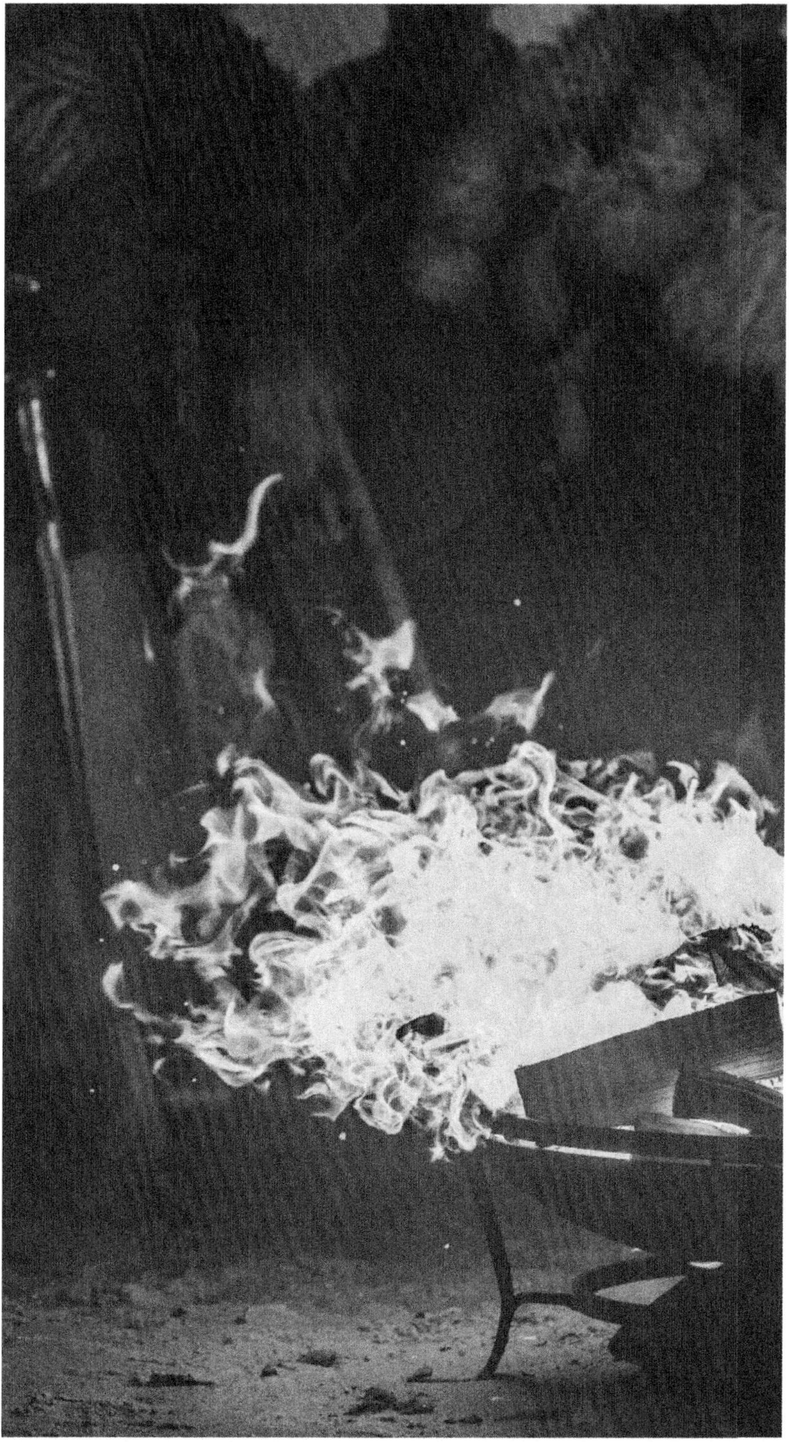

CHAPTER 3
GEOGRAPHY AND REGIONAL CUISINE

• • • • ● • ● • • •

Viking geography might seem like a difficult or complex subject as it covers such a vast range of greatly-differing territories. However, it is vital to be aware of what impacted the Viking culture in terms of the climate, terrain, geographical features, and oceans that surrounded their home. These geographical factors played a crucial role in determining how the Vikings lived and how they impacted history. Each one of the different regions in Scandinavia and other places Vikings lived played their own role in determining how that culture thought and functioned. Most critical of all, perhaps, is understanding how the Vikings made use of sea routes in the expansion of their empire, and how this would lead them into contact with the rest of medieval Europe. The ramifications were to be enormous not only for that time but for centuries to come. Let us start by familiarizing ourselves with the geography of the different regions where the Vikings lived, and the names of the important places and locations in their history.

Where the Vikings Lived

The Vikings were located all over the Scandinavian region at first. Their original territory stretched from Norway in the north and west (a larger region), to Denmark in the south (a smaller territory), and to Sweden further east. There were no major roads between these territories, and thus travel was severely hampered, as was trade.

Also included in the Viking territories were Iceland, the Faroe Isles, the Baltic coast, and Normandy. The Vikings travelled all over the globe: They invaded Europe, the British Isles, the Eastern half of Europe (modern-day Russia, Ukraine and these surrounding regions), the Middle East and Persia, North Africa, and even stretched as far as North America. One could say that their reach was truly global in this regard.

Terrain

The Viking's land was inhospitable and rocky. There was little welcome for travellers to that land. All around them was ice and snow, and also the unfriendly sea. Seeking a more fertile land, the Vikings decided to leave this desolate place and seek greener pastures further south. Better farmland was available in southern European countries and the British Isles. Although wood was plentiful in Scandinavia, there was a lack of fertile soil that they could use to grow crops. Also, the climate wasn't ideal for growing the many types of crops that the Vikings needed. In these times, it must have been customary to make do with whatever one had, but it was hard to ignore the fact that there were more fruitful places elsewhere.

Natural Wilderness

The natural wilderness of these Scandinavian countries was rough and unforgiving, as mentioned before. There were many forests, icy caves, gorges, and ravines. It was a picturesque land, but it was not friendly to those unaccustomed to its ways. It was the ruggedness of this terrain that eventually convinced even the Vikings to move and search for better and more hospitable territory.

Climate

The climate in Scandinavian countries is widely familiar. Ice and snow dominated during the winter months, and even during summer there could be inclement weather. Viking people had to be prepared for anything, and they learned to endure the very worst of conditions. This meant that when they migrated to the milder climates of southern European countries, they were accustomed to the weather that sometimes flared up in these places as well. The only thing that the Vikings needed to do was to adjust their culture and ways of living to suit the new climates and environments they found themselves in.

Ocean

The ocean played a vital role in the development of Viking civilization. It was used by them for numerous activities, namely the transport of their men on raiding missions. It was also an important facilitator of trade routes, and was an important way that the Vikings could migrate between the southern

European countries to expedite their economic activities. The oceans bordering Viking territories in Scandinavia were the Arctic Sea to the west and the Baltic Sea to the east. Further to the south was the North Sea and even further south than that was the Mediterranean ocean. As the Vikings expanded further southward, they opened up new trade routes for themselves, and eventually ended up making the long trip west across the Atlantic to find the New World. Vikings also travelled as far as the Adriatic, the Black Sea, and even further to the Caspian Sea on the borders of the Asian continent. Elements of Viking culture continued to influence much of Eastern Europe for centuries to come.

Plants and the Environment

When speaking about the geography of Viking times, one cannot ignore the way in which the Viking people interacted with nature and their environment. What did they think about the world that they saw around them and the natural world specifically? Nordic people in general and Viking people in particular took great pride in their gardens, and they also took a great deal of interest in the environment itself. They tended to make use of whatever they could find to grow if it could benefit them in some way. A garden in a Viking town might have consisted of many different kinds of plants, herbs, and flowers depending on the social status of the people who owned the garden. The art of horticulture dates back many thousands of years and has always fascinated ancient civilizations. The Vikings were no exception.

With the constant back and forth movement of Vikings from their countries to Europe, they took back many herbs, seeds, and flowers. Some of the fruits and vegetables that Vikings used in their gardens included onions, cabbages, turnips, peas, beans, watercress, plums and apples, different kinds of flax used for making fabric, and many others.

Viking gardens are noted for their small, square shape. These tiny intimate gardens can still be seen dotting the Norweigan countryside as a long-forgotten sign of a bygone era.

Viking Foods in Different Regions

Viking civilization itself is a fascinating mix of traditions, rituals, and cultures. And no more is this more apparent than in their daily lives. What did the Vikings eat? How did they live? The answers to such questions are thought-provoking and offer an insight into the often-overlooked details of their lives.

Viking food was determined largely by where

groups lived in the different regions of Scandinavia. Because there were people from such divergent regions spanning a landmass the size of a large country or a continent, foods would have differed substantially.

Due to the fact that the Vikings lived in a cold climate, they needed all the food they could get, so that they could maintain their body fat and stay warm during the cold, dark winters they faced. The Vikings cared little for what might be termed "fat free" food or "healthy food." They were not about dieting. Meat, fish, cereals, berries, milk, honey, alcohol, and fruit and vegetables were all part of their diet. Let us look at the way the Vikings ate in more detail to get a better understanding of how their culture worked. Why were mealtimes important to the Vikings?

Food wasn't always available to the Vikings. It had to be grown, caught, gathered, or hunted. Vikings needed to be self-sufficient. This could sometimes be difficult when resources were scarce. We can tell a lot about what the Vikings ate by looking at the remnants of what were once their homes, in the fragmented bones and fragments left behind in the ruins of their towns and cities. We can also read the literature that they wrote and get a better understanding of what they ate.

According to Rouă (2016), the colder climates played a role in what kind of food was eaten. Vegetables are used to a lesser extent in Nordic cuisine and the preservation of meat is noted in some of their recipes, because it was easier to store. Norway was noted for this. On the other hand, in the Danish region, soils were far more effective for growing crops, and pork was eaten instead of fish.

A Typical Viking Meal

According to "Viking Food" (2019), a typical Viking meal is described in the poem about Hárbard and Thor, where Thor meets Odin who is disguised as a fisherman. He describes the meal of oatmeal and fish he ate before leaving home. This seems consistent with what we know about Viking food preferences. They ate a lot of berries and grains because these are the kinds of things they grew in the regions where they were living.

Let's look at other foods Vikings ate during their meal. It goes without saying that nuts and berries were the foundation of the Viking diet.

Raspberries, bilberries, blackberries, plums, walnuts, hazelnuts, and wild apples were all gathered by them. Apples were considered to be particularly healthy ("Fruit and berries in the Viking age," n.d).

The Vikings kept much in the way of livestock. They usually would have pigs, goats, sheep, cows, horses, hens, geese, and ducks. All of these animals could either be used for their meat or eggs. Sometimes they would be used for their milk. The Vikings made the best use of their animals. First, they would be used for their milk, or used as pack animals or for labor. Next, they would be slaughtered and killed, their bones, skin, and horns used for clothes, implements, and cutlery. If a cow was considered too worn out to work anymore, it would be slaughtered and its meat used for months in advance—depending on the size of the cow.

One of the problems that the Vikings faced during their time was the preservation of food. This could be overcome by salting meat or fish, thereby preserving for months or even years. Because the Vikings lived close to the ocean, they had their pick of many different kinds of fish. One of the most popular kinds of fish was herring.

The Vikings also made use of the offal of

animals to make sausages, stew, and stuffings. Horses were also consumed on some special occasions.

The Vikings drank milk and also made cheese or butter. Salt was added to butter to make it last longer.

One of the most common foods was, of course, bread. Bread formed the staple of life during the Viking age, especially the dark and coarse rye bread. Oats, millet, and barley were also considered to be of great importance, as they could be used in many different kinds of dishes. Wheat was a luxury to the Vikings due to the problem with growing it in their harsh climates. Flatbreads were made with a mixture of rye flour, honey, eggs, and water. These were grilled over the fire because ovens were an unknown invention to the Vikings at this time; they would only become popular much later on.

Porridge was a popular Viking food because it was easy to prepare, cheap, and nutritious. Various kinds of grains and cereals were used to make porridge and many different kinds of ingredients could be added. Buckwheat, oats, and millet could be combined with fruit to make a healthy breakfast. Berries and apples could be added to sweeten the porridge even further.

Porridge was considered to be one of the foods that poorer people ate.

Alcoholic beverages were considered some of the most popular items in a Viking diet. Beer was one of these. It was created using barley. Water wasn't always safe to drink and thus it was avoided sometimes. Watered-down beer was drunk by both children and adults, and those who were unused to drinking hard liquor. The Vikings were very fond of mead, and it played a large role in their culture and traditions. This spiced wine was mixed with honey and drunk in large quantities at weddings and other celebrations. Wine was made with fermented grapes. It was a luxury that only a few could afford.

Vikings loved hunting, and would hunt and kill many strange kinds of beasts for their food. When livestock was scarce, there were always other animals that they could use as food, such as wild game and wild birds. These birds included pheasants, partridges, and many other kinds of fowl. Wild game included elk, reindeer, and even bear. Their fur was made into rugs or used as clothing. The Vikings did not like to waste anything that they got from their kills while hunting.

A popular image of Vikings is that they cooked

their meats over a large open fire using a spit. While this might have been the case in some instances, it is thought that the Vikings weren't overly fond of roasting or frying their food. One of their favored methods of cooking was boiling. In fact, one of the most famous Viking dishes, called *skause,* was a combination of different kinds of meats and vegetables that were added day after day until the flavor was rich and intense. It was served with a coarse bread made of all kinds of grains, and even sometimes ground tree bark was added for nutritional value. The Vikings would make sourdough bread using old leftover dough mixes, and would even add buttermilk or fermented milk to their breads to give it a tangy flavor. By doing so, they enriched their breads greatly.

The Vikings grew many different kinds of vegetables. White carrots were added to the *skause* pot along with peas, beans, and endives. The Vikings grew cabbages and also grew herbs and spices. These included cumin and coriander. In the event that they were unable to grow something, they could obtain these spices from local trade and markets although at great cost. Condiments such as horseradish sauce and mustard sauce were also very popular amongst the Vikings.

Inspection of remains of Viking homes and sewers revealed that they also sometimes inadvertently ingested poisonous weeds and husks. Evidently, Vikings must have made themselves ill from time to time by eating whatever they could find, and from making bread from flour ground from these inedible weeds.

The Benefits of a Viking Diet

A Viking diet was high in essential fats, vitamins, and nutrients. It relied greatly on fish, red meat, and vegetables with an abundance of whole grains and alcoholic beverages, much the same as what is known as the "Mediterranean diet" today. It gave the Vikings plenty of energy for the tasks that they needed to carry out.

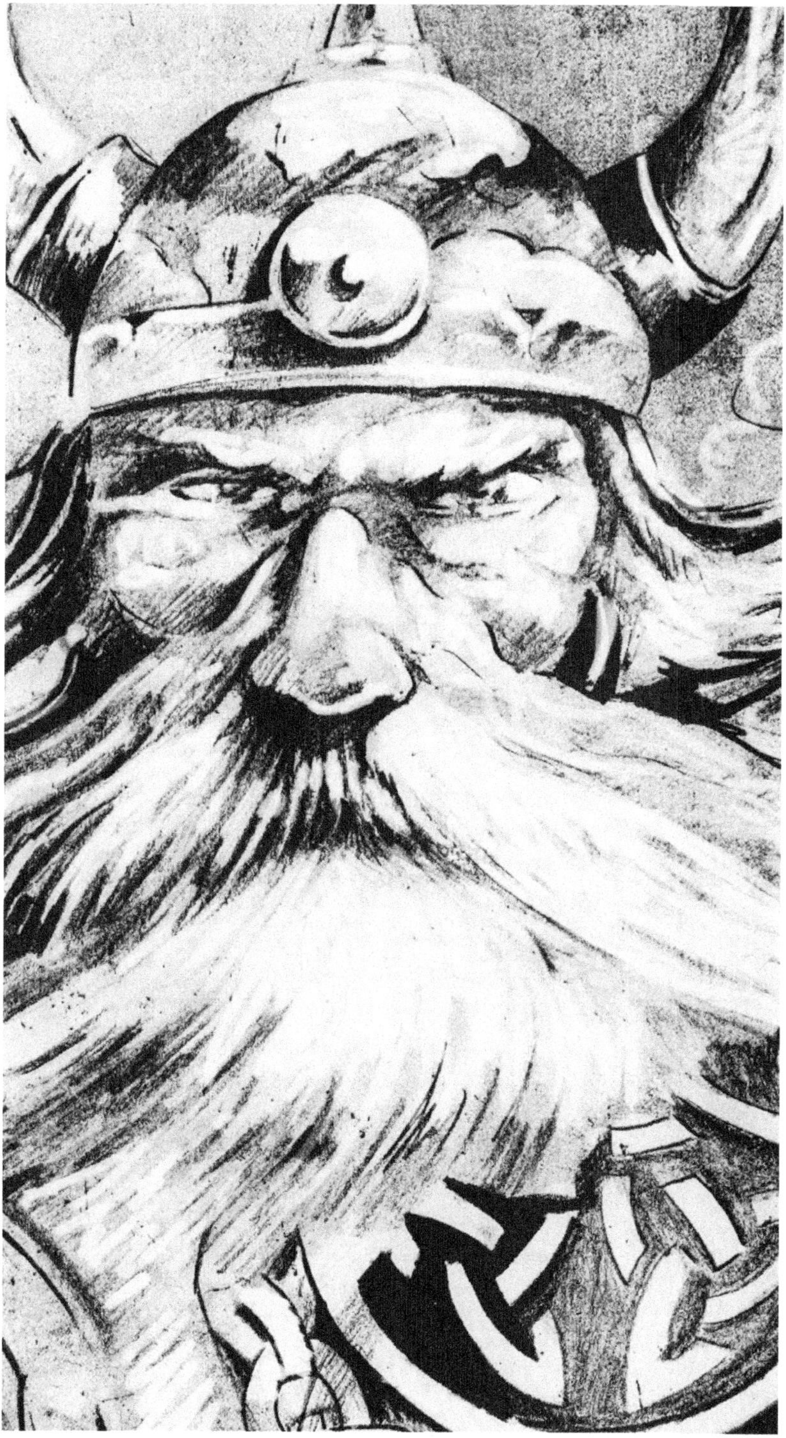

CHAPTER 4
BELIEFS, MYTHS AND MYTHOLOGY

In order to understand how the Viking mindset works, one must understand that they viewed everything through a naturalistic and also a mystical perspective. The events in the natural world that they could not explain would simply be put down as the interference of supernatural origins beyond their ability to control. The following chapter is a brief overview of their basic understanding of the world as they saw it. Some of the names may seem strange or unfamiliar, but bear in mind that these names are reflective of a language and a time period long ago forgotten. It is only through understanding these cultures that we ourselves can begin to connect to the past in a meaningful way and learn from it.

The Beginning of the Universe

The Vikings believed that the universe began with two distinct elements: Heat and cold. When these two elements met each other, the great frost giant, or titan, 'Ymir' was formed. 'Audhumla,' the primeval cow of Viking creation mythology, licked and suckled Ymir, and in the process created 'Buri', who would go on to be the father of the mighty Odin himself. Audhumla also created 'Vili' and 'Ve.' These three gods went to kill Ymir and use his body to create the earth and his head to create the sky. One of his eyebrows was used as a barrier to prevent the world of men, or Midgard, from interacting with the world of the giants (more commonly known as titans).

At the centre of all creation stood a grand tree known as 'Yggdrasill.' Its roots spread to all corners of the universe: One root spread to Asgard, or the home of the gods; the next root spread to Jotunheim, or the realm of the frost giants; and finally the last root spread down to Niflheim, or the realm of the dead. The tree connected all worlds in the Viking universe and was considered to be the most sacred of objects to the Vikings. It was populated by various strange beasts, birds, and animals that could talk to each other. In order to understand this world, it is necessary that we get acquainted with the main characters of the story: The Viking gods and goddesses themselves.

Viking Gods and Goddesses

The following is an account of the main players in Viking mythology. This list is by no means exhaustive and is meant to introduce the reader to the way which Viking mythology works. Everything is intertwined and so it is important to understand these basic characters. The story builds on itself. It is worth noting that there are two groups of gods: The *Æsir* and the *Vanir*. The first group are the principal gods and the second group are the lesser-known gods.

Odin

Odin is probably one of the best known gods in Viking mythology and is the name many think of when they hear the term "Viking god." He was considered to be the king of all the gods and the ruler over them. He is noted for wearing an eyepatch, as a reminder of the sacrifice he made at the well of *Mímisbrunnr*, one of the wells which stands near the tree Yggdrasill. The other two wells are *Hvergelmir*, the home of a giant serpent and *Urdarbrunnr*, the well of fate which is guarded by three Norns. Their names are Urd, Verdandi, and Skuld. What happened at the well of wisdom was that Odin desired the water from it so that he could continue to grow in wisdom and knowledge. So determined was he to gain this knowledge that he offered to give his right eye in order to take one drink from it. And so it came to be that in Viking culture, Odin became the symbol of all-seeing wisdom in the form of self-sacrifice.

Frigg

Frigg was the wife of Odin and was considered a lesser being than him. However, she was still considered to be the queen of the goddesses. She is thought to be the second most powerful of all the gods and goddesses because of her rank and status as Odin's wife. She was also the goddess of marriage, and her name means 'love' in the ancient Viking tongue.

Tyr

Tyr was the god of war and battle. He was known for his bravery and courage in combat. A truly fearless leader, he lost his arm to the great and terrible wolf Fenrir. He was also the god of treaties and justice. Being as they were, a warlike people, the Vikings honored *Tyr*, as he was seen as an embodiment of all that they stood for: Expansion, conquest, bloodlust, and battle.

Loki

Loki is commonly known as the trickster god in the many books that are written about Norse and Viking mythology. But he is a vastly more complicated character in mythology than is commonly shown on screen and in TV series. In Viking literature, he is also known as the god of fire. Loki is commonly depicted as having arcane magical abilities but in reality, his tricks stem from the fact that he is able to shape-shift at will, becoming anything he wants to be. His rank in the Viking god hierarchy is uncertain, and his power level amongst the gods seems inconsistent due to his portrayal differently in different kinds of Viking literature. What is known, though, is that he is the uncle of Thor and son of Fárbauti. He has a few strange myths and legends attached to his name, one of which is the fact that he gave birth to Odin's mighty eight-legged horse known as Sleipnir. Loki is also depicted in much of literature as a troublemaker, who often involves himself in schemes that not only embarrass others, but also himself. He is without a doubt, one of the most misunderstood, but fascinating gods in Norse literature.

Thor

Thor is the hot-tempered relative of Loki, and the son of Odin himself. He is a symbol of strength in Viking mythology, and he is also the god of thunder—capable of feats of incredible power. He is considered one of the strongest of the Æsir gods. His name means 'thunder' in the ancient Teutonic languages. However strong Thor may be, he does have a tendency to make rash and impulsive decisions, and this is shown within Viking literature.

Frey and Freya

Frey and Freya begin the list of the lesser pantheon of gods in the Viking belief system. They were brother and sister and were considered to be the symbols of fertility within Viking mythology. They were about equal in terms of their power level. Their role in the pantheon is not always clear, but they were made honorary members of the *Æsir* pantheon due to their special role in being a symbol of battle, fertility, and sex. Their presence seemed to create some form of tension between the two pantheons, which is told of in the Viking sagas themselves.

Aegir and Njord

Aegir and Njord are considered to be gods of the sea and oceans. Aegir, the god of the deep sea, is negatively portrayed in Viking literature, and seems to be hated and feared by the other gods and by people because of his tremendous powers. One of his brothers is in fact, the legendary Loki himself. Aegir was depicted in literature as having white hair and wave-like paws, as befitting his 'sea-like' form. He was universally despised because of his actions at sea. When a ship would overturn, he would gather the treasure for himself. His house, thought to be to the west of Midgard, was full of treasures, and he lived in great luxury. As with all the gods, there are many stories told about him in these Viking sagas.

Njord was considered to be the guardian of people who travelled via the waterways. He was also considered to be the god of summer, fishing, wealth, and the more positive aspects of the sea.

Bragi

As the son of Odin, Bragi was considered to be one of the wisest gods in the pantheon. His gift was being creative with words and making artistic constructions out of them. As well as being the god of poetry and stories, he is also the god of song and lyrics.

Ull

Ull was the god of archery and weaponry. He was skilled in individual combat and proficient with the bow and also with skis. He was a great warrior, as well.

Hel

The final goddess in this list is the goddess Hel. She is also known as the goddess of death. There is a distinction between the place in Viking mythology called 'Hel' and the goddess herself, who inhabited and ruled over this realm. She is tasked with receiving the dead as they arrive in the underworld—a similar role to Hades in Greek mythology.

Paganism in Viking Culture

Paganism in Viking culture involved the worship of the natural world and everything that could be perceived with the eyes. The Vikings saw the mystical in everything around them. Supernatural origins were given to phenomena that they couldn't easily explain by natural means. It's helpful, in this case, to look at examples of where the Vikings saw strange occurrences in the world around them, such as the changing of seasons. Lacking a scientific understanding of why seasons changed, the Vikings might have believed that good and pleasant weather was a blessing from the gods. When it was inclement, the adverse was true, and someone must have done something to anger the gods. While little is known about the practices of the Vikings as far as their beliefs are concerned, there is some material which discusses the mythological side of this belief system. What material we have comes from Viking literature and the sagas. The reason for this is because the Christian church and medieval writers suppressed much of the original material about these beliefs, seeing them as being evil in origin. A key factor to remember about Viking religion is that it was not an institutionalized set of practices. Rather, it was a set of beliefs practiced by people in their homes, in the way that they saw fit. According to *Pagan Religious Practices of the Viking Age* (2009), an example of this personalization in religion was when traders in Sweden once made sacrifices to their gods on an island in the Black Sea under a large oak tree in order to give thanks for a safe and fruitful voyage on the river Dnieper. This ritual was not done with any other group of people at that time.

The sagas do, however, tell of large and ancient temples in Iceland. They are described in great detail, however, the measurements seem improbable going by real-life standards. It seems more common that Vikings, if they wanted to worship their gods, set up their own personal backyard shrines and made use of those. Religion, it seemed, was an intensely personal thing. Everyone had his or her own way of doing things. They might keep any number of important and sacred objects within the shrine such as small bowls, armrings, and other items of worship.

Although it has been noted that Viking religious customs were a personal issue, there did seem to be a handbook that gave certain regulations for how to practice the various belief systems. This text is known as the *Landnámabók*. It was meant to give guidelines on what to keep in the public shrines, and directives on what to do when swearing an oath on a sacred ring. It seems that these rings played a large role in Viking pagan practices. Failure to adhere to the rules could anger the gods and incur their wrath and punishment. Chieftains themselves were required to wear the rings at sacred ceremonies and during sacrifices. There are also records requiring a tax to be paid to temples, the same as would have been paid to churches in other European countries.

Trees were a common symbol in Viking pagan belief systems, and temples were often set up next to them or under them. This might have had to do with the fact that the great tree Yggdrasill was at the center of the universe.

The word *vé* appears on many different Viking place names throughout the ancient Viking world. It is a shortened form of the Norse word *vígja*, which means to consecrate. Where the word appeared, it meant that the place was in fact holy and therefore could not be desecrated. Special rules governed the spilling of blood here. If a person spilled blood in this place, their place in the society of Vikings would be forfeit, and they would become an outcast. How this form of consecration took place or what these places were for is unknown.

In the 10th century, Olaf Tryggvason became the king of Norway. He imposed Christianity on the Viking people by destroying their idols, burning their temples, and taking the sacred rings. With the advent of Christianity in Scandinavia, these practices no longer had a place in Viking society and within a hundred years or so, they all but ceased to have been practiced.

Christian Beliefs in Viking Culture

The advent of Christianity changed Viking society forever. Religion became an institutionalized normality, and there were expectations placed on the people of Viking towns. Many were forced to accept Christianity or face some kind of sanction. Viking sagas tell of a group of farmers living under the rule of King Olaf in the 11th century. They lived in the Fjord region of Norway, and kept a small idol filled with bread and meat, which they offered to the gods each day. The king found out and was very angry, confronting the farmers one night and causing their ships to be damaged and their horses to run away. At dawn, the farmers approached him carrying their idol. As they walked towards him, the king stated that the sun would rise with a great light, and it did so. One of the king's men then struck the idol with a heavy club, causing it to break and the contents to spill out. The king pointed out that the idol had no power because it had been broken. The terrified farmers, looking at their ships filled with water and their horses running away, had no choice but to accept Christianity there and then.

It seems that in spite of the advent of Christianity in Viking culture, there were some who still tried to practice the two belief systems concurrently. Records of these incidents are included in the Viking sagas.

The Sagas and What They Tell Us

It is worth investigating these sagas and seeing what they reveal to us about the Viking mindset. They are probably the best and most complete resource that we have, and they give us great insight into life during the Viking age. The following accounts give some brief examples of Viking practices, from their construction of pagan shrines and temples to their practices. Also included in these sagas is the way in which Christianity impacted the Viking system of pagan worship.

Accounts of Pagan Practices in Viking Sagas

In chapter 15 of the *Vatnsdæla* saga, there is evidence of Viking temple construction and use. Although the Vikings valued individuality within the context of their religious beliefs, this did not stop the building of these often impressive structures. One well-known settler by the name of Ingimundur Gamli constructed a temple in the picturesque Vatnsdalur valley. As he was busily digging the holes for which the pillars that held up the structure would be placed, he discovered the amulet of Freyr, which had been prophesied would happen by a seer before he left the shores of Norway.

Another example of the Viking dedication towards building temples for their gods is seen in the *Kjalnesinga* saga. A man by the name of Þorgrímur built a temple at Hof and placed an image of Thor inside it. Also in the building was a fire that never went out, a copper bowl for collecting blood for sacrifice, along with a number of oath rings. Outside the door was a pool into which the bodies of people who had been sacrificed were hurled.

The Viking belief in human and animal sacrifice was steadfast, as grim as it may seem. Accounts of people and animals being sacrificed to the gods exist in the Viking sagas. It was important for Vikings to be on favorable terms with the gods, and for this to be the case, a steady supply of blood had to be provided to them. Accounts of animal sacrifice are found in Haakon the Good's sagas, which were written by the well-known documenter of Viking experiences, Snorri Sturluson, much later in the 13th century.

To begin with, a story is told about animal sacrifice. A man named Sigurd Håkonsson regularly made sacrifices to the gods. It was a common practice amongst farmers to gather at the temple and to give their grain and animal offerings. Animals were butchered, and their blood was collected in small bowls and with twigs. It was then sprinkled on the altars, walls, and over the people themselves. The meat was then boiled in large pots or cauldrons and eaten in celebration. Glasses of beer were carried around the fire in the room, which were then blessed by the chief worshipper, also called a 'magnate.' These cups were passed from person to person. Toasts were made to Odin and to the Viking king. At the end of the feast, Sigurd Håkonsson covered the costs of the feast himself.

But what of the idea of human sacrifice? Could the Vikings sanction something so bloodthirsty by our standards? The answer is to be found in the idea that the Vikings valued human life very highly. To them, to give a life to the gods was no small matter. It was one of the most costly gifts that they could provide. Written sources do tell that Odin demanded human sacrifices. How did these sacrifices take place and what was the context surrounding them?

A German monk from Bremen wrote an account in 1072 of a meeting at Gammel Uppsala, where a sacrificial ritual was carried out in order to dedicate the temple to the gods. According to his writings, nine male animals (of different kinds) and nine male humans were sacrificed. The number nine was seen as mystical to the Vikings. At the end of the ritual, the bodies of the victims were hung from trees. Speculation abounds as to whether this account (and many others like it) are true. This is due to the fact that the monk never witnessed the killings himself, and it is likely linked to Christian propaganda after the turn of the millenium, due to the fear that they had of Viking practices. However, it is a fact that there are accounts of Viking human sacrifice littered throughout the sagas and Viking literature. Much still has to be learned about the way in which the Vikings approached these practices and the value that they placed on human life.

Viking Mythology and Folklore

Much can be found within the stories that are written in Viking literature, both fictional and non-fictional. These stories not only tell of the Viking gods and their exploits, but also of the people they watched over. These stories entertain, amuse ,and make us question aspects of our lives. Viking mythology is some of the most diverse and interesting in the world due to the multitude of perspectives it appeals to. It is still popular to read these stories even to this day. Apart from the gods we have already encountered, it is also important to note some other significant characters in the Viking stories.

Heimdall

Heimdall was the gatekeeper of the 'bifrost', in the great and glorious realm of Asgard. The bifrost was the rainbow bridge that connected Asgard to the other nine realms, including Midgard or Earth. His role was to ensure that no evil thing entered the realm, and to keep a watch on all that went on in the other realms. He was the all-seeing eye that looked for danger and raised the alarm if there was any.

Thiassi

Thiassi was king of the frost giants in Jotunheim, their realm.

Iduna

Iduna was a goddess who is said to have possession of some apples, which if eaten, would cause eternal youth. They were regularly consumed by the gods in order to keep themselves young.

Skrymnir

Skrymnir was a noted frost giant from Jotunheim.

Fenrir

Fenrir was the name of a ferocious wolf sent by Loki at the end of all things in the time called Ragnarok.

The following stories give some accounts of the gods and their exploits. These stories only form a fraction of the many tales handed down from Viking times.

Freya and the Goblins

Freya, the Viking goddess of fertility, was exceedingly beautiful. Odin had given her a special place amongst the gods because of this beauty. One day, Odin invited her to go to a magnificent feast with her husband, Odur. Unfortunately, she discovered to her horror that she had nothing to wear. In spite of her husband's protests, she insisted that she must have a rare and expensive piece of jewelry. So, she set out across Asgard to find something interesting to wear to the party.

She hadn't gotten very far before it started raining. Worried that she might mess up her hair, she sheltered in a cave that happened to be conveniently placed. Once inside the cave, she started to hear hammering sounds. Who could it be? Further down the tunnel, she could see a light shimmering. As she went closer, she saw that it was a massive cavern! And encrusted on the walls of the cavern were precious stones of every shape and sort—gold, silver, diamonds, emeralds, rubies, and sapphires. What she also saw were hundreds of tiny little men beating hard at the walls with their picks and shovels, trying to extract the precious stones. They were the goblins—evil, mean, and cruel little creatures—and greedy to boot.

However, as cruel as they were, they were very skilled at making stunning jewelry. Some of them were clustered around a table, looking at something. It flashed as bright as the sun and shimmered against the cave walls. As she approached, drawn nearer by the stunning light, they all turned to look at her. She saw that they were holding a necklace of great beauty. With evil grins on their wicked little faces, they said, "Welcome Goddess Freya!" They offered to give her the necklace, at a price. "What was the price?" she asked. "A kiss for all of us!" they answered. At first, she hesitated, repulsed by the thought of kissing all those grimy little faces. But she wanted that necklace so very badly she was willing to do anything. So, she kissed each one of the hideous little faces and then grabbed the necklace and ran out of the cave, all the way back to her home where she met her husband Odur.

Feeling rather pleased with herself, she showed the necklace to her husband. "How did you get it?" he asked sternly. When she replied and told him all she had done, he grew pale with rage and shame. He ran from the house over the rainbow bridge and was gone. Freya was heartbroken and told her tale to Odin, asking him if she could return the necklace to the goblins. But he refused, saying that she was to wear it for eternity as a curse. As she was nursing her grief, an unexpected helper came to her—the trickster god Loki. He noticed that she had been crying and that she wanted to get rid of the necklace. He, too, was fond of jewelry. He waited until she was asleep in her room, took the form of a fly, and flew in and landed on her pillow while she was sleeping. Turning himself into a bird, he grasped the necklace in his beak and flew out of the window with it.

However, he forgot that Heimdall could see everything that went on in the city of Asgard, and didn't realize that he had been spotted by him.

Heimdall rode after Loki shouting, "Stop thief!" But Loki refused to stop. "You'll have to catch me first!" he called. And with that, he said the magic words and turned himself into a fireball. But Heimdall was unimpressed. "Do you think you are the only one with magic powers?" he responded, and turned himself into a rain cloud, drenching Loki and putting out the fire. Grabbing the thief, Heimdall took the necklace from him and went before Odin. "Shall I return it to Freya?" he asked Odin. "No," Odin replied. "She has learned her lesson. Return it to the goblin cave and tell her husband it is time for him to return."

Thor Against the Frost Giants

Thor was noted as the mighty god of thunder, and there were few who dared cross his will. However, one day, he had an encounter with some titanic creatures and learned a valuable lesson from the experience. One day, Thor, the god of thunder, went to Odin and announced that he was going to the land of frost and ice to pick a fight with some frost giants. Loki was with Odin at the time, who thought the matter a merry affair. Nonetheless, he consented to let Thor go on the adventure, and Loki went with him. Setting off in Thor's chariot which was pulled by two goats, they crossed the rainbow bridge all the way to the land of Midgard, where they halted before a rickety, broken down cottage. They knocked on the door and asked if they might stay the night. What little food the villagers had was set before the gods, and it wasn't very nice, but then Thor had an idea. Raising his hammer above his head, he brought it down on the head of one of the goats, killing them. So, with meat now provided, they all sat around and had a merry meal of goat stew.

Now Thor had expressly forbidden anyone at the table to crack open the bones, but Loki ignored him and told the villagers that they could do what they liked. So, the unwitting villager cracked open the bone he was eating and sucked out the marrow that was inside. When it came to the end of the meal, they all lay down to sleep. The next morning, Thor once again raised his hammer over his head, said the magic words, and all at once, the goats were back to their normal selves. Except, a part of one leg of one of the goats appeared to be missing, and that goat was now limping around. "Loki!" roared Thor, knowing at once who was responsible.

So, they continued their journey to the frost giants' country, all the way to the mystical land of Jotunheim. All at once, they found themselves there and a huge mansion stood before them with a peculiar round opening in it but no door. Thor entered through the doorway, confidently followed by the others. They found themselves in a room with a large open hallway and five small narrow rooms at the end of it. As they settled down to rest for the night, they felt a massive shaking beneath them, like the sounds of an earthquake. An eye appeared in the round doorway they had entered through. A large voice called out, "What are you doing in my glove?" They realized that they were in a giant's glove and the narrow 'rooms' at the end were where the fingers went. With a roar, Thor flung himself at the giant and struck him on the head with his hammer. But it had no effect on the giant. He simply yawned and said, "Someone's throwing acorns at me again." Even angrier, Thor threw the hammer at the giant's eye, with the same result. "Oh dear, there seem to be a lot of flies around today. One just flew into my eye," the giant said in a bored voice. Now absolutely enraged, Thor struck the giant on the skull with all his force, the hardest blow he could muster. "Oh dear, it seems like some bird has done his droppings on my head," the giant lamented, not at all bothered. He let out a hearty laugh and strode away. The giant, whose name was Skrymnir, said as he was leaving: "Farewell my friends! Tell your king how you tickled Skrymnir today." But Thor was determined to go after him and defeat him.

Following the giant's footsteps, which were very large, Thor and Loki arrived at a large and stony cavern, and found there a number of giants feasting, sitting in a circle. "It is I, Thor, god of thunder!" Thor announced. They all looked at him, including Skrymnir. "Oh, it's you again?" he looked at Thor quizzically. "Well, what do you want?" he asked. "To feast with you before I do battle with you," Thor answered. "Do you think you're fit to feast with us?" they asked him. "I can drink like no other god in Asgard," Thor answered. "Very well," they answered. "Drink this cup empty and we will believe you're stronger than us." It was a cup shaped like a horn with a wide mouth and a point at one end. But try as he might, Thor could not finish the liquid in the horn. He drank and drank and still the horn was filled to the brim. Eventually, he had to give up. He had failed the first challenge. "No matter," said Thor. "I'll beat you in a feat of strength." "Very well," the giants replied. If you can lift our cat off the ground, we'll believe you're stronger than us." The cat was very large, belonging, as it were, to a giant. Try as he might, Thor could not lift the cat off the ground, only managing to lift a single paw. He had failed the second challenge. Finally, he said, "Enough! This time I will beat the strongest of you in hand-to-hand combat." The giants agreed to this and sent for the goddess Hel to wrestle with Thor. When she arrived, Thor was insulted. She was a tiny, shriveled old woman. So they wrestled. Before Thor could even cry out, she had him on the ground and pinned, and he could not move a muscle. Three times he had failed, and he now accepted his defeat. Before he left, Skrymnir said that it had all been by magic. You see, the reason why Thor could not finish the liquid in the horn was because one end is dipped into the sea and the sea can never be overcome. The reason he failed the second challenge was because the cat was not a cat at all, but a serpent who's tail wrapped around the whole earth and could never be dislodged. The reason he failed the third challenge was because, being death itself, Hel could never be beaten by anyone. No one can win against death.

Enraged, Thor aimed a mighty blow at the head of Skrymnir, but the giant only laughed mockingly and disappeared into thin air before they could move, leaving the two gods speechless and ashamed.

The Apples of Iduna

One of the most well-known stories in Viking

lore is the story of how Iduna was abducted, and the gods had to go and rescue her. It was a well-known fact that Iduna was the goddess who kept the apples that were the secret to eternal youth. Every day, the gods and goddesses of Asgard would eat the apples and grow a little younger. In this way, they were effectively immortal and immune to aging. One day, Odin decided to go on a trip and he took Loki with him. While they were waiting for the daily meal which was being cooked by Loki, Odin looked up and saw a bird sitting in a tree outside. It said, "Give me some of your stew and it will cook faster!" The two gods were surprised, but the bird kept repeating the same words over and over. Loki attempted to strike the bird with a big stick, but it grabbed the stick and started to carry Loki away. The bird's name was Thiassi, but he was really a frost giant.

Eventually Loki cried so hard that the bird said, "Give me something and I will put you down in return." Loki agreed to this and then asked the bird what he wanted. "Revenge on the gods," it answered.

"Why?" Loki asked. "I don't know yet," answered the bird. "Help me find out." Loki took the bird to Iduna's garden. He called Iduna and told her that he had seen some apples that were better than the ones in her garden. He asked her to come with him, but she refused, saying that the gods might be in need of the apples. Eventually, though, he persuaded her and she came out carrying her basket. But as they were leaving, a voice from the treetops called out, "Don't go, Iduna!" Thiassi swooped out of the sky and grabbed Iduna, carrying her into the sky. Loki watched her go from the ground. She was gone for two weeks. However, with Iduna gone, there were no more apples of youth. The gods started to age, including Loki. So, they had to make a plan to get her back.

At this time, the all-seeing Heimdall went to Odin and told him that he'd seen Loki, Thiassi, and Iduna together. From this it was easy for them to discover what had happened. Odin was very angry and promised to punish Loki when he returned from rescuing Iduna. Loki turned into a falcon and sped towards the frost giant's castle. He sat on a window sill and listened to Iduna and the frost giant talking. He wanted the magic apples. He took all of them that were in Iduna's basket, but as soon as he touched them, they shrivelled up like little peas. Frustrated, he threw the basket back at her and said that she would be locked up forever. Loki flew into the room and turned into his normal shape. She was not pleased to see him, but eventually he convinced her that they needed to go back together. He turned her into a sparrow and her basket into an apple pip. Turning back into a falcon, he flew with her all the way back to Asgard.

However, the angry Thiassi had followed them and turned himself into an eagle. He followed them all the way back to Asgard. "What are we going to do? cried the little sparrow. Odin saw them coming and commanded that every twig and branch be gathered. Loki and Iduna saw that Heimdall was on the ground building a big fire. As the flames from the fire started to leap higher and higher, they heated the wings of Thiassi. He crashed to the ground while Loki and Iduna changed back to their original forms and were unharmed. The basket of apples also turned back to its original form. The gods could finally taste the fruit again, and return to their younger selves. Thus ended the story of Loki and his flight with Iduna.

These are some of the tales of Viking lore. They give insight into a truly unique and interesting culture.

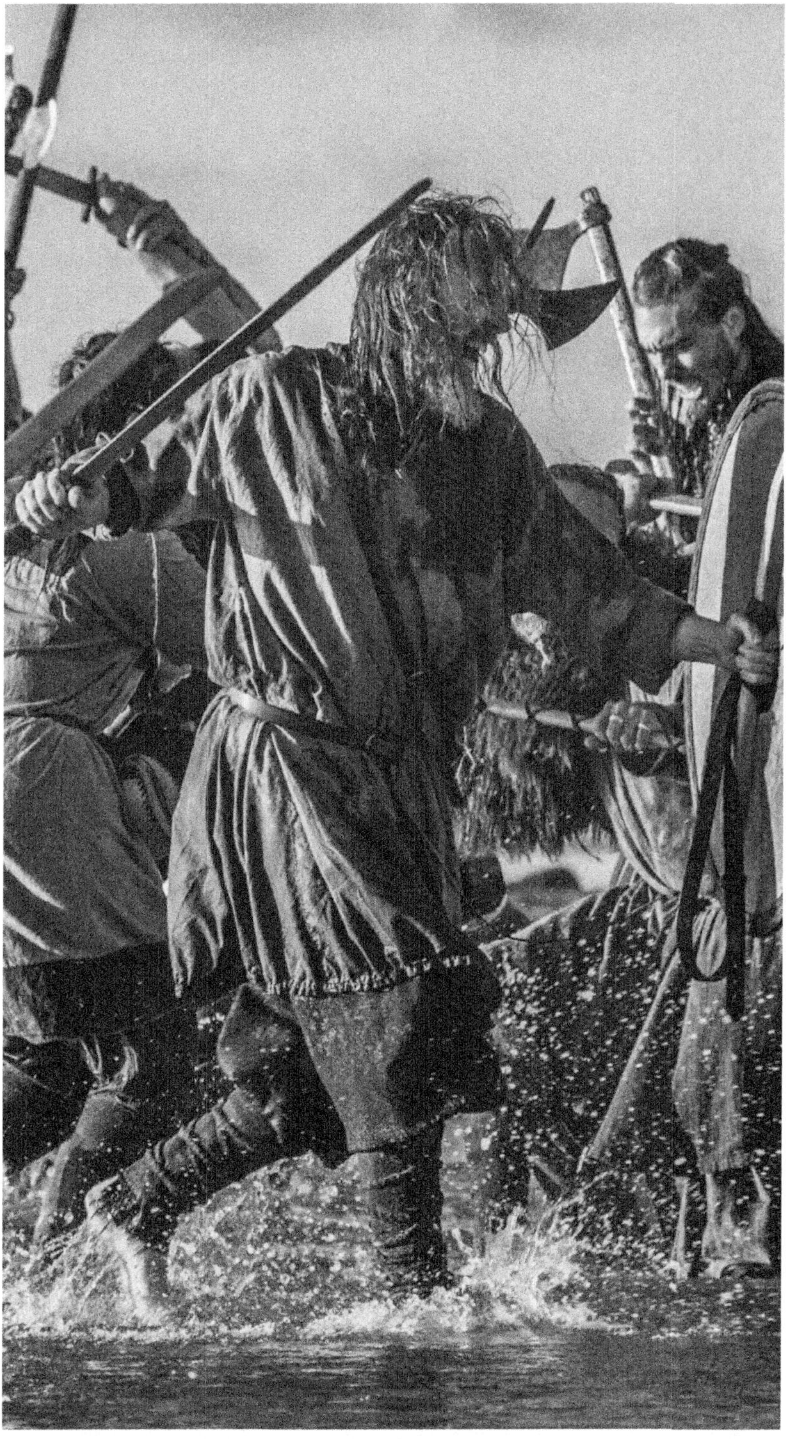

CHAPTER 5
THE VIKING ARMY AND FAMOUS BATTLES

How Did the Vikings Fight?

If there was one thing that the Vikings were known for, it is the fact that they were great warriors. In fact, their military prowess is considered to be the stuff of legend. Viking warriors were not noted for their tactical acumen, and it was not on par with some of the best armies in the world at that time, but they were unparalleled in individual combat. Their awe-inspiring troops operated on the principle of fear, and this gave them the mental edge in battle. So magnificent were Viking warriors in battle that they were often thought to have mystical powers with the way they fought.

Viking troops did not fight in formation usually, although they did make use of some rudimentary formations. This may have been because they were not educated enough in this style of warfare to make it effective. Their movement was described as being like bees swarming all over the enemy and overwhelming them before they could recover or realize what was happening to them. These tactics were especially effective against the small, unarmed towns they often came into contact with.

One of the most well-known types of Viking troops was called a 'berserker.' This was a kind of warrior which was said to have been imbued with the power of the gods. They seemed to be almost immune to physical injury on the battlefield, and were known for entering sudden rages that would render the enemy helpless against their onslaught. Hence, the name 'berserker.'

One of the reasons that the Vikings were so successful on the battlefield is that they ignored much of what was thought to be conventional military discipline and tactics. Instead, they relied on their emotions to guide them in battle. Vikings were not above using any and every tactic to win a fight, including using deceit and subversion. Their mentality was a win-at-all-costs one. This is evident in literature detailing the history of the battles that they fought.

Vikings on the Ocean

One of the areas where the Vikings thrived most of all, of course, was the ocean. They were unparalleled in naval battles and their longships did not seem to be troubled much by the navies they encountered—even some of the most powerful navies in the world. Viking naval combat was swift and deadly, often known for its ambush-style tactics. The Vikings could be the aggressors and attack directly, but they could also be subversive and wait for the enemy to come to them if they needed to. A common tactic seemed to be that they would beach their ships and attack the beach and the forces on it en-masse, almost like a resisted landing in modern warfare. Vikings would attack the beachhead, or other area, using a wedge-like formation with the best troops stationed at the front.

The Great Heathen Army

After around 865 AD, the Vikings formed into a more organized army unit, composed of men from different regions of Scandinavia and Denmark primarily. The aim of this coalition was a targeted assault on the Northern English territories. Before this coalition was formed, the Vikings had only been making sporadic assaults on various monasteries around the coastlines of various European countries. This force, however, was much larger and aimed to seize and capture territory with a long-term focus.

The name "Great Heathen Army" was taken from a set of chronicles written in 865. The expedition was led by the four out of the five sons of a chieftain named Ragnar Lodbrok. Their names were Halfdan Ragnarsson, Ivar the Boneless, Bjorn Ironside, and Ubba. The timeframe for the existence of this coalition and its activities lasted for about 14 years.

The large invading force first landed at East Anglia, where they were given horses and promised to spare the inhabitants of that region. After dwelling at Thetford for a number of months, they marched north to capture York. York had belonged to both the Romans and, much later, the Anglo Saxons.

During 867, the group marched into Mercia. After agreeing terms with the Mercian army, the group moved back to York in 869 but returned to East Anglia much later on and killed the king there. In 871, they invaded Wessex, where they were given money to leave by Alfred the Great. The next seasons were spent reinforcing their already formidable ranks in preparation for an attack on Mercia. In the years that followed, Mercia was overrun. After the king of Mercia fled across the ocean, it seems that the group divided itself into two groups: One went to Wessex, and the other went to Northumbria. In May 878, the Vikings were finally overcome and agreed to peace terms with Alfred the Great. They would be allowed to settle in Northern England and establish a more permanent presence there.

The size and composition of the group is a matter of debate. Sources claim that a raiding party would be around 35 men. This was the smaller 'unit', as it were, of the Viking army. The Viking king issued a proclamation that any party smaller than this number would be considered a raiding band, and not part of the main army. This was to differentiate between the larger and smaller Viking forces.

As for the Viking ships themselves, they were of the smaller variety and could carry around 35 men. These smaller ships had their advantages and disadvantages. They could slip into enemy waters unnoticed and were far quicker than anything the European forces could muster, which gave them a huge advantage in battle. By this, historians have concluded that the average Viking fleet could consist of about 1,000 men, far smaller than anything they could face. But they had the advantage of morale and training. During the Viking raids on various European countries, they augmented their forces by forced conscription and by paying off men to join their army.

The invasion started in 865 in East Anglia. The Vikings were offered money by the people of Kent in return for peace, but they raided and pillaged the area anyway. Further invasion of British regions followed, and the Vikings installed puppet rulers in these places, such as in Northumbria in 867.

In 871, a large force called the "Great Summer Army" arrived in Wessex and engaged the forces of Alfred the Great, where they were defeated. It was one of the first major military reverses of the Viking age, and it brought with it a new understanding of how their forces could be tamed. In the wake of these battles, the Viking group split into two and settled in two distinct parts of England. They became farmers and started to establish themselves as a presence there. Further victories over the

Vikings by Alfred the Great in 878 meant that these newer groups of warriors had to sign peace treaties and accords with the people living on the land. It was agreed that the Vikings should take portions of English territory for their own, and boundaries were clearly demarcated between these territories.

In the aftermath of repeated conflicts in the late 9th century, King Alfred realized the value of having a strong navy and set about the creation of it. It is possible that this realization and the beginnings of the British navy would set the scene for their naval dominance over the next thousand years. The English navy would always be known as one of the strongest in Europe, if not the world. Their proximity to the water made this a necessity, and the Viking raids only served to underline the importance of this fact.

King Alfred also fortified the coastal cities and generally strengthened English defences, cleverly making use of old Roman cities that were already strong. Because of the speed of Viking raids, Alfred the Great needed a force that could be quickly mobilized—and so a standing army was created. By the 10th century, it seemed that the Viking raids had all but ceased, and the strength of their army shattered.

They were still a latent threat, but the fortitude of yesteryear was gone. Broke and without leadership, many migrated to Europe and settled there while others spread out from their cities of Northumbria and East Anglia. They did still, however, control much of Northern England. The Vikings, on the whole, saw no real reason to keep expanding into the British and European territories.

So, how did the Viking army fight and what were their weapons like? The nature of Viking warfare was to attack quickly and to get out as soon as possible. Viking terror started with the very nature of their attacks. The way they attacked was unexpected, and they used the cover of darkness to hide their movements. Their ships were specifically designed to cut through the water as smoothly and with as little friction as possible. The lightness of their ships made it so they could traverse shallower waters, and therefore they were able to access areas with their ships that were difficult. The mobility of the Vikings was not a new trait in warfare. It had been used by many civilizations before them, such as the Huns way back in the 5th century. The idea of raiding and then getting away was still a new phenomenon to many conventional armies.

Viking hardware or weaponry was dependent on the sword, shield, and axe. These were their main tools, and they had the strength to use them well. Attacks were not a free-for- all as are commonly depicted in the media. Instead, they were carefully planned and executed. Viking attacks could be planned for months in advance and were meticulous in nature. The Viking steel was of an exceptionally good quality and stood up well during the rigors of battle. During the siege of Paris in 885 onwards, the Vikings made use of siege weapons such as catapults, battering rams, and other projectile-based weapons. This showed that far from being just a raiding force, they also had understanding of how to plan and prepare for longer battles.

But far from just the physical side of combat, the Vikings also held the edge mentally. They lived in a violent warrior culture that glorified battle and victory. So, they were always ready to go to war. Let us look at the way in which the Vikings were trained militarily, as this will show why they were able to accomplish great feats in battle.

As in any army, there are different classes of military professionals in the Viking regiments. Although they were unconventional in their style of warfare, they still kept organized in different groups of soldiers, from the most experienced and dangerous to the least professional. Training was everything to Viking warriors and they pushed themselves hard in battle. Training could include running, swimming, jumping, various physical activities such as lifting heavy weights like rocks and logs, and many other kinds of disciplines. For specific kinds of Viking warriors, different kinds of exercises were required. They learned how to move and attack as a group, how to defend in a shield wall (a noted tactic of Viking warriors), and many other defensive and offensive disciplines.

More wealthy Viking warriors could have men under their command. These groups of men were known as *hird*. The bigger a man's *hird* was, the more wealthy he was seen to be, and the more influential he was. He could be seen to be someone who was capable of protecting himself and everything he owned. These groups of men practiced in the pig's snout formation, which was a wedge-shaped arrangement used by the Vikings. It was meant to crack open enemy lines with the narrower point of the wedge. The shield wall was also widely practiced, but this was more of a defensive maneuver. Vikings would train by actively pushing against opposition shield walls (amongst themselves). By doing so, they strengthened their forces, and gained a sense of the resistance needed in order to hold back the enemy during the battle.

From a young age, Vikings were trained to be battle-hardened and ready for war. It was necessary to instill the proper techniques that they would need in later years. Young boys and children got used to using their weapons before they became men. By the time they were grown, they were proficient in using many different kinds of weapons due to their long years of training. They became experts in using swords, spears, shields, bows and arrows, and axes. All of these weapons required their own special kind of training and innate skill to be able to master them, and it was considered essential for a Viking to master both offensive and defensive techniques. Due to the Viking way of life and the savage nature of their culture, many did also die young. Life expectancy during this time must have been much lower for the Vikings, as opposed to other cultures where war was not glorified in such a way. But to the Vikings, death was just another adventure in their journey.

Famous Viking Warriors

In a culture such as the Vikings, military figures and warriors feature highly amongst some of their most famous people ever. This does not mean that there were not other people of high status in Viking culture (i.e. kings, nobles, royals, artists and writers). However, being an expansionist culture, men who went to war held a special status. What follows is a list of some of the most notable people in these wars and what their accomplishments were.

Ragnar Lothbrok

Ragnar Lothbrok is considered to be one of the most influential figures in Viking history. He was a great warrior and military commander during his time. He frequently led men on raiding missions of the English and European coastlines. At some point, he attempted to invade France and was offered 7000 lbs of silver to turn around and leave by the Frankish King Charles. He met his demise while on a raiding mission off the English coast in around 852, although there is a debate about the date of his death. He attempted to assault English forces with just two Viking ships and was captured, being subsequently killed by being thrown into a pit filled with vipers.

Rollo of Normandy

King Rollo was one of the first Norman kings in France, and left an indelible mark on French, Viking, and European culture. In 911, he signed treaties with the king in France, which allowed the Vikings to settle there. Included in the deal was the provision that he would protect France from any further Viking raids. He died in 928, and his son William Longsword took his place. His descendents, the mighty Normans, were responsible for invading English in 1066, leading to significant changes in English culture for centuries to come.

Egil Skallgrimsson

Egil Skallgrimsson was a complicated figure in Viking lore due to his complex personality and volatile nature. He was a true artist and was responsible for creating some of the most beautiful poems in all of Viking literature. From a young age, he was a violent and brutal individual, killing another boy at the age of just seven. His tumultuous nature carried on into later life, and he was part of prolific raiding teams. For a period of time, he had a blood-feud with another great warrior king named Erik Bloodaxe, who sent men to kill him and his son. However, Skallgrimsson killed every man who was sent to assassinate him. When he was eventually taken captive, he appeared before Erik Bloodaxe and constructed a poem of great beauty and emotion. So impressed was the king by his poetry that he decided to spare Skallgrimsson's life.

Cnut the Great

Cnut the Great was one of the greatest warriors in Viking history. He was responsible for conquering most of England in 1013. After his father's death, Cnut made treaties with King Edmund of England and was allowed to remain there. After King Edmund's death, he assumed leadership of the whole of England. During and after his rule, Scandinavia experienced a period of stability and flourished greatly. He died in 1035 and his son Harthacnut took over until his own death in 1042.

Harald Hadrada

Harald Hadrada led possibly the last major Viking incursion into Europe, namely England. He is most noted for conducting the Viking forces at the battle of Stamford Bridge. He could be considered to be the last of the truly great Viking chieftains. His name means "hard ruler" in the Viking language. As a young man, he spent time in Eastern Europe and worked as a mercenary there. Later, he joined the prestigious Varangian Guard in the Middle East. After gaining wealth and power, he returned to Scandinavia and ruled Norway with the help of Magnus the Good. He then became embroiled in a battle with Svein Estrithsson, which ended with Hadrada giving up his right to the throne, and instead focusing on defeating the English instead.

He invaded England in 1066 and won a great victory at the battle of Fulford Gate. Encouraged by these early successes, he decided to push the assault even further. He faced the English forces under the leadership of Harold Godwinson, and was overwhelmingly defeated by him, leading to his death during the battle. Harold Godwinson himself would be killed a short time later at the Battle of Hastings against William the

Conqueror. These battles marked the end of the Viking raids on England and Europe.

Bjorn Ironside

The son of Ragnar Lothbrok, Bjorn Ironside inherited his father's ruthless nature and desire for conquest. He is noted for his triumphs in Southern Europe and the surrounding regions. According to *12 Famous Viking Warriors You Should Know* (2020), one of his most notable victories came when he infiltrated the town of Luna, pretending to be dead. When his men took his apparently lifeless body inside the city, he jumped out of the coffin and fought his way through towards the gates, where he let his men inside, leading to a glorious rout of the enemy. He continued to raid, pillage, and plunder for many years after this. But one day, during a battle, things went wrong, and he lost 40 or more ships during a single skirmish. After this incident, he retired to Sweden where he saw out the last of his days in ease and comfort as the king of that region.

Erik the Red

Erik the Red is most noted for being one of the first Europeans (if not the first) to land on the shores of Greenland. He was ruthless, violent, and had a dangerous temper. After his father was expelled from Norway for killing a man, he went to Iceland where he lived out his formative years. However, after killing several men himself, he was expelled from Iceland, and decided to take on the life of a nomad. Returning to Iceland several years later, he recruited several hundred men and set sail for Greenland where he established a colony there. His son, Leif Erikson, was the first man to reach the shores of the New World, or as we call it today, America.

Ivar the Boneless

Ivar the Boneless was the father of the noted Ragnar Lothbrok, one of the most influential figures in Viking military history. He led the Great Heathen Army to York, where they overcame the forces of King Edmund and settled there. His unusual name came from the fact that he was born with a condition that rendered his bones more liable to break than that of other men. Hence, his reputation as a great warrior was well-earned.

Famous Viking Battles

Vikings took part in many battles over the course of their history. Some they won, and some they lost. But they always fought bravely and to the last man. Examining these battles gives an insight into the Viking way of fighting and the tactics they used. It helps us to understand their mindset in battle. The following list gives an account of the most famous Viking battles in history, and also highlights how each battle shaped and was shaped by the historical context it was fought in. No battle is ever fought in a vacuum. There is always a political and historical context to every conflict. Let us look at Viking battles that shaped history.

York

The Battle of York was fought in around 866, when a massive force known as the Great Heathen Army attacked the kingdom of Northumbria and took it over. One year prior, the people of East Anglia had sued for peace, but it was not to last long as the Vikings came back in even greater numbers. The Vikings took advantage of the element of surprise they had over their hapless victims and massacred them in the freezing English winter, when they were least prepared for it. This battle marked the last rites of the Northumbrian kingdom, and the Vikings effectively established a presence in the North of England.

Englefield

The Battle of Englefield was fought in 870 between the Vikings and the inhabitants of the town of Reading in Berkshire. These men were West Saxons. Before this, the Vikings had been inhabiting Wessex. The Vikings marched towards Englefield, led by the Viking leader Sidrac. Aethelwulf of Berkshire was the leader of the West Saxon forces, and led his men to a hard fought victory over the Vikings, who retreated with heavy losses.

Ashdown

The town of Reading was once again in the spotlight in 871 when Viking raiders sailed down the Thames and took over the town of Reading. At this time, feast days were being celebrated by British soldiers. It was, in fact, Christmas, and everyone on the English side was in a merry mood. The English army mobilized but were pushed back as far as Englefield where the Vikings followed them. Unfortunately for the Vikings, the British forces fought back and routed them. They attacked them again and were again defeated by the great leader Alfred, who was only 22 years old at the time.

Edington

Edington was an early battle in the Viking age between the Viking and English forces. It represented one of the major English reverses over the Vikings, at that time when they seemed so dominant. The Great Heathen Army attacked the forces of Alfred the Great at Wessex. The Vikings encountered an unexpected defeat, and the Viking leader Guthrum agreed to be baptized and converted to Christianity at that time.

Maldon

The Battle of Maldon was fought between the Vikings and the West Saxons around the year 991. The commander of the Saxons was called Ealdorman Byrhtnoth, and the Viking commander was called Swein Forkbeard. The West Saxon commander approached the battle with far fewer forces than the Vikings and was soundly defeated, having to pay the victorious commander 10,000 Roman pounds of silver in tribute.

Stamford Bridge

The battle of stamford bridge represented the end of the viking age and the end of their military might. It was fought between the english forces of king harold ii, and the viking forces of harald hadrada from norway. In 1066, the viking king was killed along with most of his army. The english cavalry won this battle in overwhelming fashion, and crushed the idea of viking invulnerability forever. There would be other battles, but it was clear that the vikings were not the force they once were. Their reign of terror was over.

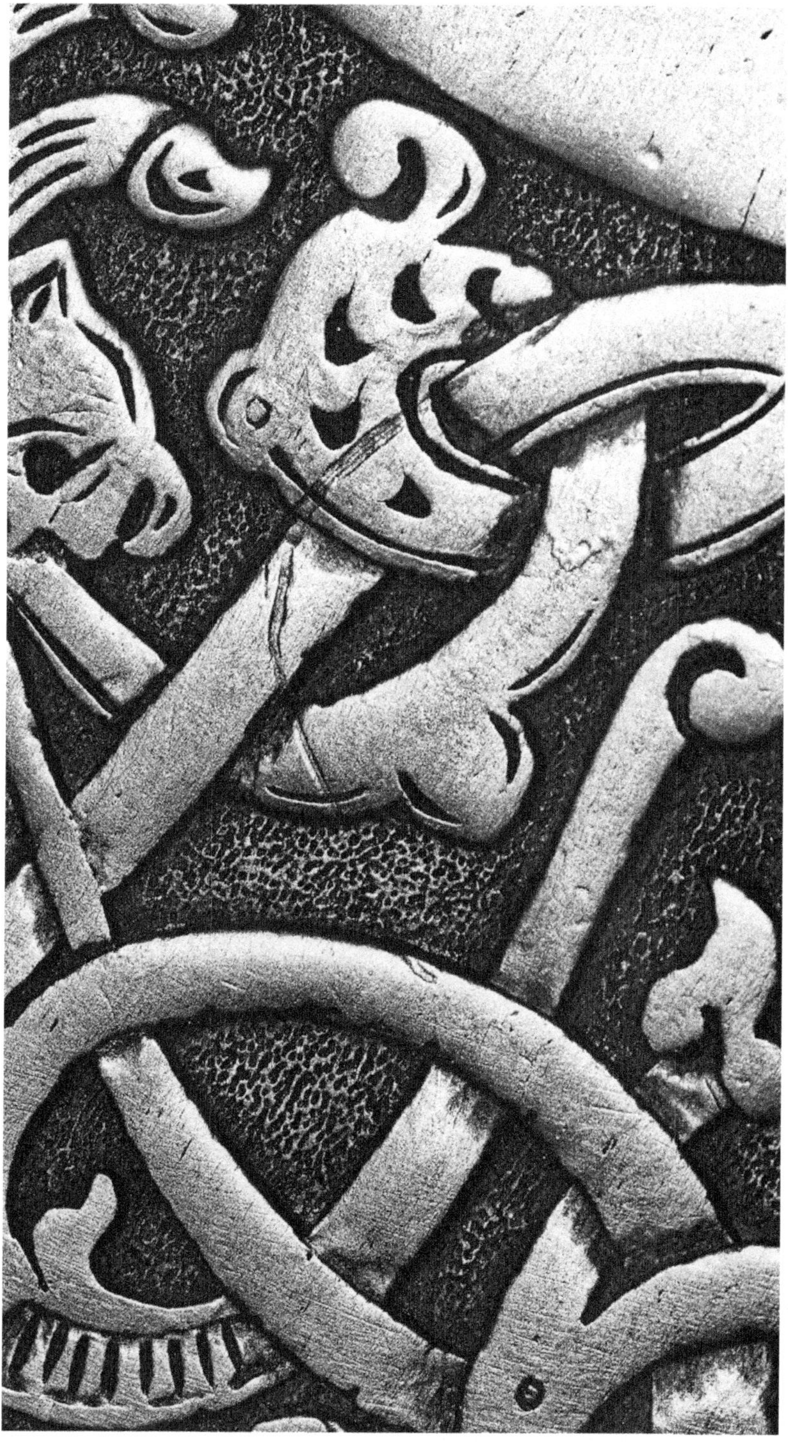

CHAPTER 6
VIKING LANGUAGE

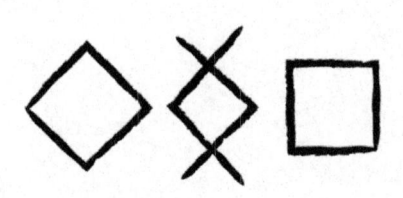

Out of all the evidence of the Viking age that is left behind, there is one crucial element that many people miss, that is the most important piece of history we have about the Vikings. It stays with us in our speech and it impacts the way we communicate with others. It is the Viking language itself, passed down from generation to generation in many forms. We still make use of the Viking language today, in modern times, especially in English. There are little traces of the Vikings in the way we speak to each other.

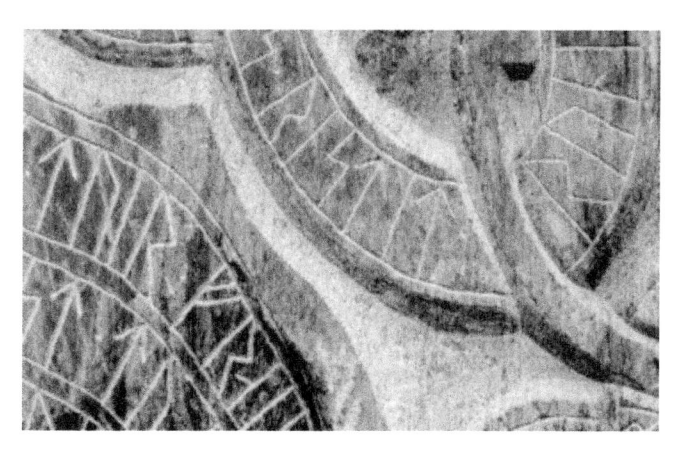

What Was the Viking Language Like?

What did the Viking language look like? It surely looked nothing like what we have today in our own modern languages. It was written in a completely different script and would be impossible for us to decipher nowadays.

Nonetheless, there are similarities in some instances. Certain words sound alike and sounds have been passed down through the centuries. But what did the Vikings used to write with? What was their alphabet like? We have the answer: They used runes. These runes were symbols that the Vikings used to communicate with each other through the written word. Let's look briefly at how these runes work. Each symbol represented a specific sound in the Viking language, just as our own alphabet represents different sounds in English. However, runes went beyond just the written sound, to being symbolic of mystical elements in Viking culture. Vikings made use of runes as a way of warding off evil and in spells and rituals. By using runes, they believed they could heal people, imbue objects with magic properties, predict the future, protect themselves or other people, and conjure curses or blessings. Their literature, including the sagas and famous poems known as 'Eddas', were all written using runes. Runes were used all across Scandinavia and in Iceland as well. It is worth noting that the Vikings spoke many languages using different scripts, but the one that most people talk about is Old Norse. Let us look a little more closely at Old Norse and what it looked like.

Old Norse

Old Norse was a Northern Germanic language. It had its roots predominantly in Northern European countries—and in Western Europe as well—just after the time of the Roman Empire. Old Norse was used in Scandinavia from about the ninth to the thirteenth century amongst the Vikings. The name of the language that came before Old Norse was known as 'Proto-Norse', and this was spoken before the eighth century. There were different types of Old Norse, or different dialects. Let us look at some of these dialects. There were three main ones: Old West Norse, Old East Norse, and Old Gutnish ("What language did the Vikings speak?" 2019).

Old West Norse came out of Old Icelandic and Old Norweigan. It was spoken in the British Isles, Normandy, France, and areas of Scotland. Old East Norse was spoken in Denmark and Sweden, as well as further East in what would eventually become Russia and Ukraine. Old Gutnish was an obscure language that was heard on the Swedish island of Gotland. It has its roots in Old Gothic, which is a language now extinct in Germany. The written form of Old Norse is called the 'Runic' language. Following on from Old Norse, we have the more modern Icelandic, which came to prominence after the ninth century, and which still continues to be used to this day. More forms of Icelandic are influenced by Danish and Gaelic. Old Icelandic is the language which formed much of the writings by famed Scandinavian historian Snorri Sturluson. Anglo-Saxon is another language that has its origins in Old Scandinavian languages. It came before Old English, and has its roots in Celtic and Latin, as well as other Germanic languages. One of the best known Anglo-Saxon works is the famed text *Beowulf,* which many still read today. Another work which is closely associated with Finnish, Old Norse, Anglo-Saxon, and Old English is the work of J.R.R. Tolkien, more specifically his critically acclaimed series of books called *The Lord of the Rings*. The languages used in these books closely mirror the patterns of old Scandinavian and Germanic languages from the Viking period. These patterns can be seen in the way the Elvish (Quenya, Sindarin) and Dwarvish (Khuzdul) languages are constructed in the novels.

Below is a verse from the Poetic Edda, *Völuspá*, stanza 19 (The Poetic Edda, 2019). The language is Old Norse.

> Ask veit ek standa,
> heitir Yggdrasill,

hár baðmr, ausinn
hvíta auri;
þaðan koma döggvar,
þærs í dala falla,
stendr æ yfir grænn
Urðarbrunni.

One immediately recognizes a few things about the language in this poem. What immediately jumps out is the name Yggdrasill, or the name of the great tree that stands at the center of the mythical Viking universe. The translation of the poem is as follows (The Poetic Edda, 2019):

There stands an ash
called Yggdrasill,
A mighty tree showered
in white hail.
From there come the dews
that fall in the valleys.
It stands evergreen above
Urd's Well.

From what this poem tells us, we can deduce that it is introducing one of the Viking stories in the sagas and is setting the scene for what follows. One can also note the naturalistic imagery that is used in the poem. The only names that one might not understand if one was an outsider are the hints to specific items or places within Viking mythology, such as *Urd's Well*. This text shows the Viking propensity for using trees in their poems, songs, and stories. It also showed that they believed that nature and the elements had mystical powers. It gives us a lot of insight into how they viewed the world and the environment.

The most interesting thing about the Viking languages is that they have had a clear influence on our own English usage today. Many of the words that we don't even take notice of have their roots in Old Norse. If one looks at the way in which English is structured, you can quite clearly see the influence of these ancient languages on the spelling of specific words.

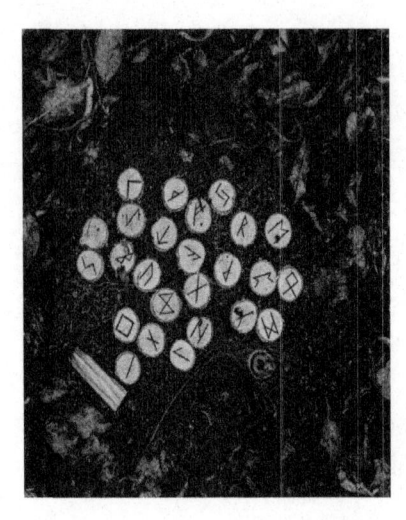

Let us look at the history and development of one specific and very common word in the English language. This word is 'wrong.' Many people wouldn't suspect that it actually originated from Old Norse, and the word *rangr*. Over time, it changed to 'vrang' in the Danish language, which eventually became our modern 'wrong.' One can see that words can evolve into different forms as time passes. The example of 'wrong' can be applied to many other words in the English language today. And language is always changing. One day, people might look back on English as we do on the ancient Viking languages and think and say the same things we do now.

Several other words that came from Old Norse are also common in the English language today. Examples of these words include: Guest (*gestr*), egg (*egg*), gift (*gipt*), want (*vant*), anger (*angra*), trust (*traust*), and score (*skor*). The names of the days of the week are unmistakably taken from Old Norse, such as the words 'Friday' (Frigg's day) and 'Thursday' (Thor's day).

The amazing thing about Old Norse and Viking languages is that there is a ton of material available for us today to learn and understand this language better.

The Viking Language Throughout History

The earliest Viking language evidence that we have is found in Denmark, in an inscription called the Vimose Comb. The Vikings were not called Vikings at this point as it was the year 160 AD. The inscription is in a runic language called "Elder Futhark."

Let us look more closely at the runic alphabet itself. It was divided into distinctive periods in which it underwent significant changes. Sometimes these periods overlapped with each other. These periods were Elder Futhark, Younger Futhark, Anglo-Saxon Futhorc, and Medieval Futhorc, the last of which appeared in around the 13th century.

Elder Futhark contained about 24 runic letters. The name of the language comes from the sounds of the first 6 letters of the alphabet. There are only a few surviving examples of this language because the inscriptions were usually carved on wood, which unfortunately does not survive over time. Thus, much has been lost to the elements. However, from what we do have, we're left with a good understanding of what this runic system was like. Some of these inscriptions are also inscribed into items such as jewelry and coins, which has survived much better. However, why these items were inscribed with the language is unknown at this point.

Younger Futhark was the written language of

the Vikings, and it is a very much more refined version of the language with a reduced number of runes. The problem with Viking writings is that because we as modern historians lack context about the inscriptions and etchings on various objects, the overall meaning of these phrases and ideas is lost. There is much that is still not understood about the Viking language and the way that they thought and acted.

Runestones

Runes are the best evidence of Viking language that we have, because they do not disintegrate, and the etchings are clearly visible to modern historians. These are very large stones with many different writings on them, found in various places throughout the Viking world. Let us look at specific examples of these runestones: One particular group was discovered in English, with a number of runic writings on them describing the Viking raids in England and their purpose there. Many tales and stories of Viking accomplishments and their victories are recorded within these inscriptions. As the influence of paganism in Viking culture faded, so did the frequency of these inscriptions. They also started to show more of a Latin influence with the advent of Christianity in Viking culture.

Poetic Edda

Another one of the best examples of Viking language that we have is called the "Poetic Edda." These poems are some of the most important resources that we have about Viking writing. These writings are a recorded account of stories and oral recollections, passed down from generation to generation of Viking families and writers. They tell of the historical sagas and adventures of Viking warriors, and other similar stories. The influences of these Eddas are widespread, and many other writers, authors, poets, and artists have made use of them in their own work, many centuries later. Let us look at some of the examples of people who have been impacted by these works. They generally tend to focus on pagan themes in Norse mythology, and so are sought after by writers and authors who are interested in these topics for their own benefit. The works of Wagner are heavily impacted by the Eddas, and J.R.R. Tolkien raided the works and used their material to influence the creation of his own fantasy world.

The Uses of Viking Language

Different forms of the Viking language had different uses in society, much like how we do in English today. They used more formal or less formal versions of particular languages depending on the social situation they found themselves in. The language that was most commonly used amongst common folk in their daily life and in informal situations would have been Old Norse. In pagan rituals and in religious ceremonies, they might have used a more formal version of the language. Much still remains to be discovered. However, one thing that is clear is that post-pagan Viking culture relied much more on the Latin influences in their language. This is clearly evident within their religious texts from the time. One way in which we can see how the language changes is to look at the way in which the references to specific pagan images changed. Allusions to items, objects, beasts, and other items not associated with Christianity naturally decreased as the mindset changed.

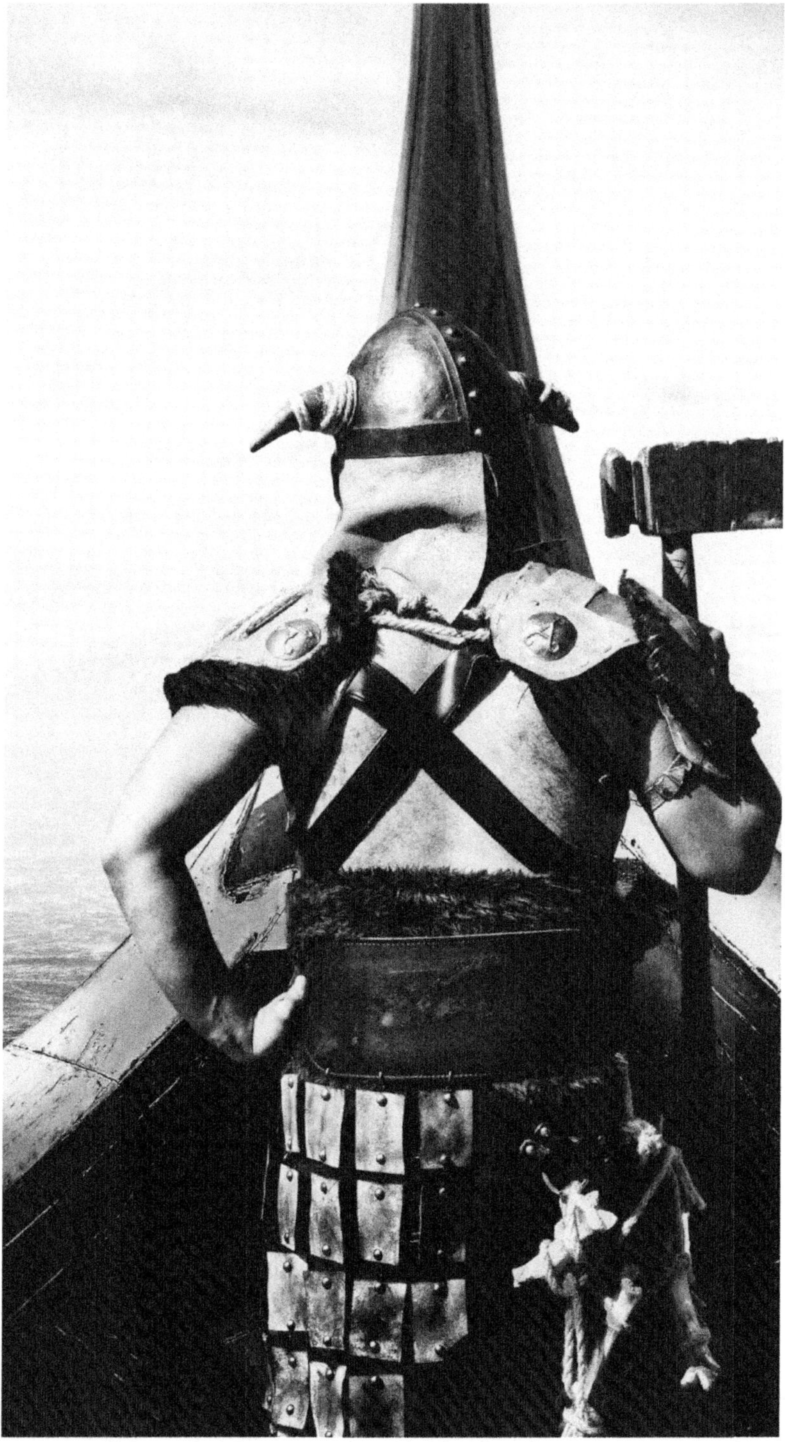

CHAPTER 7
WHAT HAPPENED TO THE VIKINGS?

The final question we should ask ourselves is what exactly happened to the Vikings? Where did their culture go, and what did they do once they started to settle in Europe? Much remains unanswered, but by examining the literature and historical evidence we have, we can learn a lot about where they went and what their eventual fate was. There are several schools of thought about what happened to the Vikings and the factors that led up to the inevitable end of the Viking age. Let us start by examining the factors that led to the weakening and fading away of their power.

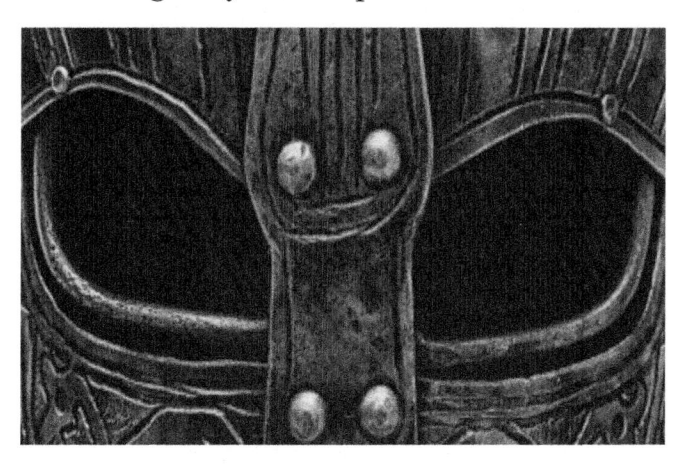

Factors Leading to Viking Decline
Strengthened Opposition

During the arbitrarily defined period from 793 to 1066, the people of Northern Europe had the greatest impact on Europe through their activities—either through their raids or through trade and industry. This is why this time is called the period of Viking dominance or Viking age. When the Vikings first launched their raids on the English and European coastlines, their presence caused great fear amongst people living in those lands. But over time, as the people of those countries grew stronger and more technologically advanced, they became more adept at dealing with the Viking raids. By the time the turn of the millennium came, the British forces in particular had strengthened greatly both militarily and on the ocean, which had traditionally been the Viking's greatest strength. Faced with more significant opposition on the sea, the Vikings could not always break through, even to make their famed raids, and thus one of their chief weapons was no longer as effective.

Weakened Viking Army

The Great Heathen Army of the 9th century could be said to be the high point of Viking dominance on the continent. It contained probably the largest force of Nordic warriors that there would ever be in a single standing army. After it split apart, it grew significantly weaker. Other smaller forces followed, but those would never be able to replicate the original army in terms of its size, organization, leadership, and strength. Periodically, the Vikings would send armies over into Britain and other countries, but they were often defeated by British and Germanic army leaders. This was because they had gotten to know how they worked and were able to counter their tactics. As they faced a shortage of funding and supplies, the Vikings were forced to adopt other tactics besides using military might.

Changing Viking Mindset

It can be said that by the time the Viking army was on the wane and no longer raiding Europe as frequently as it did in the past, Viking attitudes towards conquest had changed. To put it simply they did not seem all that concerned with expanding beyond the territories they had conquered. It is fair to say that Vikings, although weakened militarily, still controlled vast swathes of North England. They had established settlements all over Europe where they could live peacefully without needing to go to war with everyone around them. In short: They had no need to go to war, and it showed both in their actions, and in the fact that they pursued peaceful rather than aggressive means.

The Impact of Christianity

Christianity arrived in Viking culture during the time of the turn of the millennium, and it had a great impact on how they saw the world and how they felt about war and military conquest. It is also fair to say that pagan Viking culture tended to view the people they came into contact differently. Christian Viking culture sought to pursue constructive ends, and the formation of friendly trade routes and connections with other countries, regions, and cultures. This seemed to be the new Viking way, established after the battle of 1066, which is heralded as the official end of the Viking age in Europe. There would still be other battles, but Europe had turned its focus away from its Scandinavian invaders in lieu of other more serious conflicts. Christianity could be said to have 'tamed' the Viking invaders, and they held no serious ideas of making any more large scale invasions of Europe.

Changes in Social Structure

When the Vikings started raiding, they were a different society in comparison to that which they ended up as. They were largely independent communities governed by what they called 'kings' but were actually just local rulers or magnates. For the most part, every man was responsible for his own land. This meant that they could build up their resources, and they had the time to go on these raids. By the end of the age, there were no longer any of these men available. Those that remained were wealthy and privileged, preferring instead to adopt an isolationist view. Supporting a family was seen as the most important thing, not conquest. So, one could say that the Viking era died out because they simply did not have the time to be able to engage in these activities anymore.

At the beginning of the Viking age, the kings of Europe were divided, scattered and leaderless. They did not have the strong leadership needed in order to counteract these determined raids. As a result, they were decimated. But as time passed and newer and more effective leaders rose to power, they began to think of new ways to deal with the threat of these raiders, and their attacks diminished ineffectiveness.

Monasteries were initially built on the coastlines, which made them easy targets for the Vikings. Over the years, they were moved inland and fortified against attack, making them less desirable for conquest by the Vikings.

The Final Years of Viking Dominance

Absorption Into European Culture

The events of 1066 had marked the official end of the Viking reign of terror over Europe, but they had been a declining force long before this. This was due to the mass Christianization of Europe and the conversion of the Vikings who were a part of it. In the previous century, the Vikings had lost much of the territory they had won. The final nail in the coffin was when King Erik Bloodaxe was killed during battle. This meant that the English kingdoms could finally unite under one rule, which made them a much more difficult proposition for the Vikings to take on. But more than just Vikings converting to Christianity and the increased opposition they faced on their raids and conquests, the Vikings were beginning to mix into the people of Europe. This meant that they no longer had the sense of nationalism that drove them centuries earlier. They were becoming more and more like the people they had set out to conquer. They would still retain a sense of their own heritage, but they no longer had the desire to overcome and kill as they once did. A newer and more peaceable generation was being born that was simultaneously Viking and European—jointly multicultural. These final years of the Viking age experienced battles, but they also experienced something else: The formation of a different kind of Viking age. This age was one that was built on trust, friendship, trade, and partnership with others rather than all out warfare.

The Aftermath of Viking Expansion

One must also ask the question: What exactly happened after the battles of 1066 and the official end of the Viking age? Did they just stop fighting or did they carry on in their own ways? There are various schools of thought about what they did, and we also have access to historical records that help us understand this post-Viking period. The first misconception that many people have is that after the Viking empire waned, the people themselves ceased to act like Vikings, and thus disappeared from the European landscape altogether. This is not entirely true. The reality is that they still existed. Did they disappear? Not at all. They went about living their lives as they had done for hundreds of years before that. The only thing that was different was that they, collectively, no longer had the lust for conquest that they once experienced. That was gone, never to return. It can be considered that the Vikings stopped raiding the European countries because it was no longer profitable for them to do so. The Vikings were never conquered. They simply ceased their activities and went about their daily lives as they did before. They became Scandinavians as they always were before. But the memories of past glories would always be with them.

Where Are the Vikings Today?

Asking the question, "Where are the Vikings today" is really the same as asking, "What happened to Viking culture?" We can see that remnants of Viking customs still exist in many countries around the world today. There are even movements set up to mimic what the Vikings were like, in a non-threatening and friendly way. But there are people who have taken this lifestyle upon themselves. These are people who not only dress up in the garb of the Vikings and take their customs upon themselves, but are true Vikings in their attitudes, ways of thinking, and beliefs. These men and women have dedicated themselves to the preservation of Viking customs and traditions so that the ways of these people never die out. So, who are these people and what are the values that they adhere to? What does it mean to be a true Viking in today's world? Lunde (n.d), states that many Norweigans are working to figure out what their true history was about, and in the process of making these discoveries, they are finding out what it really meant to be a Viking during the Viking age.

Popular places to meet fellow Viking enthusiasts and those who have adopted this type of lifestyle for themselves are what is known as "Viking markets." These markets are not only a great place to buy various kinds of goods and services, but also a great way for fellow modern Vikings to meet with each other and build community. Many of these markets are famous in their own right, as they historically housed Viking kings of the past. Authentic village recreations are also present, faithful to the style of original Viking constructions. There are many Viking reenactment camps around Scandinavia these days. There are also many thousands of participants who take part in these camps each year as well, and many more fans of the Viking lifestyle abroad.

Children are also welcome to learn about the Viking culture and replicate the battles that the Vikings fought for themselves. With the advent of virtual reality, it is possible to feel like you're going back in time with none of the pitfalls of being a Viking. Children can immerse themselves in Viking culture to their heart's content. As one of the modern-day Vikings said, it was like combining the ancient culture with the new. People are drawn to the Viking culture because of the blood and gore and because of the battles and excitement it seems to elicit. But when we look beyond the obvious, we see that they were complex and sensitive people.

CONCLUSION

Viking culture fascinates many because it speaks to something within us that we can relate to: The fight to succeed and to grow stronger. Vikings only did what they did because they wanted to better themselves, fight for their people, and to expand their territory. Like them, we also desire things for ourselves. But if we don't go out and take what we want, we will never experience the satisfaction of knowing that we did something to improve and further our lives.

We learned that they started off with a vision and a plan, and that they were not afraid to get out of their comfort zone to go and take what they wanted. Their methods may have been questionable, but the heart and attitude of their community can never be questioned. When they achieved what they wanted, they stopped fighting for it, and things changed in their mentality and culture. What this shows is that sometimes in order to survive, you have to keep fighting for what you want. If you stop fighting, things change. And so it is with the cultures of the world.

On the opposite side of the spectrum, what their history demonstrates is that people often thought of as barbaric can undergo a shift in perception, and a change in mentality. Nothing stays the same forever. And when we realize that nothing stays the same, we will stop holding on to memories of the past. We have to allow the past to change us, but we also have to learn when to let it go.

The Vikings themselves showed incredible fight and spirit in adverse circumstances. When they were faced with challenges, they didn't simply carry on as if they believed they were invincible. They withdrew and thought about how to deal with situations they had to overcome. This is the essence of being a true Viking warrior—having the right attitude in every circumstance, having a sense of purpose and of destiny, and having the determination to fight for the things you hold dear.

The reason why the Vikings were successful was not only because they fought well. It was because they knew what they wanted, and they were not afraid to go after it. They had the utmost faith in what they were doing. Throughout their entire history, from the time they first arrived on the shores of the countries they were attacking, they had a sense of pride and certainty in what they wanted to do. In other words, they had clear vision, foresight, and understanding of their enemies. It might have had to do with the fact that they had no choice, a lot of the time. When they elected to leave their home it was a bold step, and the choices they made after that also needed to reflect this boldness.

So, overall, what we've learned from our journey on the Viking ship, as it were, is that we need to have the right attitude to succeed in life. Without the right attitude, we'll never have the strength and correct mentality to achieve what we want. Remaining where we are might be more comfortable in the long run, but this doesn't necessarily mean we will be safer. What the Vikings have proven throughout their years is that confidence breeds further confidence. If we have the right mentality, we'll never be afraid to take risks. This doesn't mean that we should make uninformed decisions, but that we should allow ourselves to be guided by the right parts of our feelings, as the Vikings did. They were successful because they used the emotion and rage bottled up inside of them to drive them to ever greater heights. The result is the fact that they will be forever remembered as a great and powerful society. The Viking era may have ended, but there is a little of their legacy in all of us. We have to take what they have taught us and apply it to our own lives. By doing so, we can tap into a little of what made them successful: Their tenacity, will to win, fighting spirit, and never-say-die attitude.

REFERENCES

Ager, B. (2001). Viking Weapons and Warfare. BBC. http://www.bbc.co.uk/history/ancient/vikings/weapons_01.shtml

Bartley, J.-A. (2018, May 20). The Ultimate Guide to a Viking Wedding. OddFeed. https://oddfeed.net/viking-wedding-ultimate-guide/

BBC. (2016, July 28). Viking Sagas (Age 7 - 11). https://www.bbc.co.uk/programmes/articles/20stJyBvh9mv7kpSVgDfKPw/viking-sagas-age-7-11

BBC Bitesize. (2019, September 16). Who were the Vikings? https://www.bbc.co.uk/bitesize/topics/ztyr9j6/articles/zjcxwty

Beer and Mead. (n.d.). National Museum of Denmark. https://en.natmus.dk/historical-knowledge/denmark/prehistoric-period-until-1050-ad/the-viking-age/food/beer-and-mead/

Bread and Porridge in the Viking Age. (n.d.). National Museum of Denmark. https://en.natmus.dk/historical-knowledge/denmark/prehistoric-period-until-1050-ad/the-viking-age/food/bread-and-porridge/

Butler, S. (2019, May 23). The Surprisingly Sufficient Viking Diet. HISTORY. https://www.history.com/news/the-surprisingly-sufficient-viking-diet

Campbell, H. (2020, January 27). 12 Famous Viking Warriors You Should Know. Viking Style. https://viking-styles.com/blogs/history/12-famous-viking-warriors-you-should-know

Christensen, C. (n.d.). Did the Vikings Have a Written Language? Get the Facts. Scandinavia Facts. https://scandinaviafacts.com/did-the-vikings-have-a-written-language/

Clothing in the Viking Age. (2019). Hurstwic. http://www.hurstwic.org/history/articles/daily_living/text/clothing.htm

Death in Norse Paganism. (2019a, May 6). In Wikipedia. https://en.wikipedia.org/wiki/Death_in_Norse_paganism

Famous Viking Battles. (n.d.). Medieval Chronicles. https://www.medievalchronicles.com/medieval-history/medieval-history-periods/vikings/famous-viking-battles/

Fruit and berries in the Viking Age. (n.d.). National Museum of Denmark. https://en.natmus.dk/historical-knowledge/denmark/prehistoric-period-until-1050-ad/the-viking-age/food/fruit-and-berries/

Great Heathen Army. (2021, May 25). In Wikipedia. https://en.wikipedia.org/wiki/Great_Heathen_Army

Great Viking Food - What Did The Vikings Eat For Over 300 Years? (2019). Medieval Chronicles. https://www.medievalchronicles.com/medieval-history/medieval-history-periods/vikings/viking-foods/

History. (2019, June 7). Vikings. https://www.history.com/topics/exploration/vikings-history

Horte, R. M. J. (n.d.). The Viking Age Geography. Vikingeskibsmuseet I Roskilde. https://www.vikingeskibsmuseet.dk/en/professions/education/viking-knowledge/the-viking-age-geography

Human Sacrifices? (2019). National Museum of Denmark. https://en.natmus.dk/historical-knowledge/denmark/prehistoric-period-until-1050-ad/the-viking-age/religion-magic-death-and-rituals/human-sacrifices/

Kjølberg, T. (2019, April 9). Language of the Vikings. Daily Scandinavian.

https://www.dailyscandinavian.com/language-of-the-vikings/

Knattleikr. (2020, January 20). In Wikipedia. https://en.wikipedia.org/wiki/Knattleikr

Lunde, M. (n.d.). The Modern Vikings. Visit Norway. https://www.visitnorway.com/things-to-do/art-culture/vikings/the-modern-vikings/

Parker, P. (2018, November 26). A Brief History of the Vikings. History Extra. https://www.historyextra.com/period/viking/vikings-history-facts/

Mark, J. (2018, January 29). Vikings. World History Encyclopedia. https://www.worldhistory.org/Vikings/

McCoy, D. (2014). Daily Life in the Viking Age. Norse Mythology for Smart People. https://norse-mythology.org/daily-life-viking-age/

Meat and Fish in the Viking Age. (n.d.). National Museum of Denmark. https://en.natmus.dk/historical-knowledge/denmark/prehistoric-period-until-1050-ad/the-viking-age/food/meat-and-fish/

Nicki. (2016, January 26). Barley honey flat-breads. Roots & Wren. http://rootsandwren.com/barley-honey-flat-breads/

Norse Mythology: Norse Afterlife. (2019, June 3). Norse and Viking Mythology. https://blog.vkngjewelry.com/en/norse-afterlife/

Norse Mythology: Viking Religion. (2020, March 30). Norse and Viking Mythology. https://blog.vkngjewelry.com/en/viking-religion/

Norwegian Vikings. (2015). Visit Norway. https://www.visitnorway.com/things-to-do/art-culture/vikings/

Old Norse (Dǫnsk tunga / Norrœnt mál). (2021, April 23). Omniglot. https://omniglot.com/writing/oldnorse.htm

Old Norse The Language of The Vikings. (2016, December 9). Verbling.

https://www.verbling.com/articles/post/old-norse-the-language-of-the-vikings-5781d9e65c69247b005203ed

Pagan Religious Practices of the Viking Age. (2009). Hurstwic. http://www.hurstwic.org/history/articles/mythology/religion/text/practices.htm

The Poetic Edda (H.A. Bellows, Trans.). (2019). Sacred Texts. https://www.sacred-texts.com/neu/poe/index.htm

Ray, D. (2018, August 21). 7 Misconceptions About The Vikings That Might Surprise You. The Franklin Institute. https://www.fi.edu/blog/viking-misconceptions

Rouă, V. (2016, April 25). Discover Denmark's Viking Age Ring-Shaped Fortresses. The Dockyards. http://www.thedockyards.com/discover-denmarks-viking-ring-fortresses/

Rouă, V. (2016, October 22). Architecture In The Viking Age: Urban Planning, Emporia, And Strongholds. The Dockyards. https://www.thedockyards.com/architecture-viking-age-urban-planning-emporia-strongholds/

Sjøgren, K. (2017, December 20). What made the Vikings so superior in warfare? Science Nordic. https://sciencenordic.com/denmark-history-society--culture/what-made-the-vikings-so-superior-in-warfare/1452248

Snow, A. (2020, October 1). Art of the Viking Age. Smart History. https://smarthistory.org/viking-art/

Útgarða-Loki. (2021, June 12). In Wikipedia. https://en.wikipedia.org/wiki/%C3%9Atgar%C3%B0a-Loki

The Viking Blót Sacrifices. (2019). National Museum of Denmark. https://en.natmus.dk/historical-knowledge/denmark/prehistoric-period-until-1050-ad/the-viking-age/religion-magic-death-and-rituals/the-viking-blot-sacrifices/

Viking Clothing: Warm and Durable. (2018, May 29). History On The Net. https://www.historyonthenet.com/viking-clothing-warm-and-durable

Viking Food. (2019). National Museum of Denmark. https://en.natmus.dk/historical-knowledge/denmark/prehistoric-period-until-1050-ad/the-viking-age/food/

Viking Games and Entertainment: Life Wasn't all Work. (2018, May 29). History On The Net. https://www.historyonthenet.com/viking-games-and-entertainment-life-wasnt-all-work

Viking raid warfare and tactics. (2019b, May 6). In Wikipedia. https://en.wikipedia.org/wiki/Viking_raid_warfare_and_tactics

The Viking Social Structure. (n.d.). Norse Mythology for Smart People. https://norse-mythology.org/viking-social-structure/

Vikings Customs. (n.d.). Medieval Chronicles. https://www.medievalchronicles.com/medieval-history/medieval-history-periods/vikings/vikings-customs/

The Vikings in the West. (n.d.). Vikingeskibsmuseet I Roskilde. https://www.vikingeskibsmuseet.dk/en/professions/education/viking-knowledge/the-viking-age-geography/the-vikings-in-the-west

What Happened to the Vikings? (2019). Hurstwic. http://www.hurstwic.org/history/articles/society/text/what_happened.htm

What Language Did the Vikings Speak? (2019, July 2). AleHorn. https://www.alehorn.com/blogs/blog/what-language-did-the-vikings-speak

Williams, G. (2011, February 17). Viking Religion. BBC. http://www.bbc.co.uk/history/ancient/vikings/religion_01.shtml

https://en.wikipedia.org/wiki/Sei%C3%B0r
Wikipedia Contributors. (2021e, July 11). Dökkálfar and Ljósálfar. Wikipedia. https://en.wikipedia.org/wiki/D%C3%B6kk%C3%A1lfar_and_Lj%C3%B3s%C3%A1lfar

FREE BONUS FROM HBA: EBOOK BUNDLE

Greetings!

First of all, thank you for reading our books. As fellow passionate readers of History and Mythology, we aim to create the very best books for our readers.

Now, we invite you to join our VIP list. As a welcome gift, we offer the History & Mythology Ebook Bundle below for free. Plus you can be the first to receive new books and exclusives! <u>Remember it's 100% free to join.</u>

Simply scan the QR code down below to join.

OTHER BOOKS BY HISTORY BROUGHT ALIVE

Available now in Ebook, Paperback, Hardcover, and Audiobook in all regions.

Other books:

For Kids:

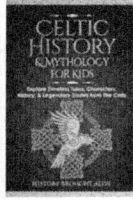

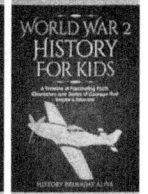

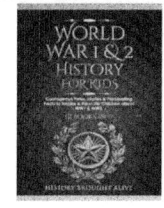

THE VIKINGS

We sincerely hope you enjoyed our new book *"The Vikings"*. We would greatly appreciate your feedback with an honest review at the place of purchase.

First and foremost, we are always looking to grow and improve as a team. It is reassuring to hear what works, as well as receive constructive feedback on what should improve. Second, starting out as an unknown author is exceedingly difficult, and Amazon reviews go a long way toward making the journey out of anonymity possible. Please take a few minutes to write an honest review.

Best regards,

History Brought Alive

http://historybroughtalive.com/

Printed in Great Britain
by Amazon